POPULATION CHANGE
AND AGRICULTURAL DEVELOPMENT
IN NINETEENTH CENTURY FRANCE

POPULATION CHANGE
AND AGRICULTURAL DEVELOPMENT
IN NINETEENTH CENTURY FRANCE

William Henry Newell

ARNO PRESS

A New York Times Company

New York / 1977

Editorial Supervision: ANDREA HICKS

———◆———

First publication 1977 by Arno Press, Inc.

Copyright © 1977 by William Henry Newell

DISSERTATIONS IN EUROPEAN ECONOMIC HISTORY
ISBN for complete set: 0-405-10773-0
See last pages of this volume for titles.

Manufactured in the United States of America

———◆———

Library of Congress Cataloging in Publication Data

Newell, William Henry.
    Population change and agricultural development
in nineteenth century France.

    (Dissertations in European economic history)
    Originally presented as the author's thesis,
University of Pennsylvania, 1971.
    Bibliography: p.
    Includes index.
    1. France--Population--History. 2. Agriculture
--Economic aspects--France--History. I. Title.
II. Series.
HB3593.N46 1977   301.32'9'44   77-77183
ISBN 0-405-10796-X

POPULATION CHANGE AND AGRICULTURAL DEVELOPMENT

IN NINETEENTH CENTURY FRANCE

William Henry Newell

A DISSERTATION

in

Economics

Presented to the Faculty of the Graduate School of Arts and Sciences

of the University of Pennsylvania in Partial Fulfillment of the

Requirements for the Degree of Doctor of Philosophy.

(1971)

INDEX

INDEX (continued)

TABLE OF CONTENTS

BIBLIOGRAPHY

Ariès, P.: Histoire des populations francaises et de leurs attitudes devant la vie depuis le xviiie siècle. Paris: Editions Self, 1948.

Augé-Laribé, Michel.: La révolution agricole. Paris: A Michel, 1955.

Augé-Laribé, Michel.: L'évolution de la france agricole. Paris: A. Colin, 1912.

Barral, Pierre.: Les agrariens francais de Méline à Pisani. Paris: A. Colin, 1968.

Bertillon, J.: France (Démographie), in Encyclopédie Dictionnaire des Sciences Médicales, series 2, volume VII. Paris, 1873.

Bertillon, J.: La dépopulation de la France. Paris: Félix Alcan, 1911.

Bourgeois-Pichat, Jean.: 20. The General Development of the Population of France since the Eighteenth Century, in Glass, D. V. and Eversley, D.E.C.: Population in History. London: Edward Arnold, 1965.

Cameron, Rondo.: France and the Economic Development of Europe 1800–1914, 2nd ed. Chicago: Rand McNally, 1965.

Cépède, M.: La mesure de la productivité en agriculture, Révue de Ministère de l'Agriculture. (May) 1959.

Clapham, J. H.: Economic Development of France and Germany 1815–1914 4th ed. Cambridge: Cambridge University Press, 1936.

Clark, Colin and Haswell, M. R.: The Economics of Subsistence Agriculture 3rd ed. London: MacMillan, 1967.

Clough, Shephard B.: France, a history of national economics, 1789–1939. New York: C. Scribner's and Sons, 1939.

Collins, E. J. T.: Labour supply and demand in European agriculture 1800–1880, in Jones, E. L. and Woolf, S. J.: Agrarian Change and Economic Development. London: Methuen, 1969.

Davis, K.: The Theory of Change and Response in Modern Demographic History, Population Index. 29:345 (Oct), 1963.

Delefortrie, Nicole and Morice, Janine.: <u>Les révenues départementaux en 1864 et en 1954</u>. Paris: A. Colin, 1959.

Depoid, P.: Évolution de la réproduction en France et à l'étranger depuis le début du xixe siècle, in <u>Journal de la Société de Statistique de Paris</u>. 89e annee, nos. 9 - 10: 206-226. (Sept. - Oct.), 1941.

Dumont, A.: <u>Dépopulation et civilisation. Étude démographie</u>. Paris: Lecrosnier et Babé, 1890.

Easterlin, R.: Does Human Fertility Adjust to the Environment? <u>American Economic Review</u>. 61:399 (May), 1971.

Food and Agricultural Organization. <u>Production Yearbook</u>, annual.

France. Institut National de la Statistique et des Études Économiques.: <u>Annuaire statistique de la france</u>, 1878+. Paris.

France. Ministère de l'Agriculture, <u>Racoltes des céreals et des pommes de terre de 1815 à 1876</u>. Paris: 1913.

France. Ministère d'Agriculture: <u>Statistique de la France</u>. Paris, 1835-52, 1855-72.

France. Statistique Générale de la France: <u>Résultats Statistique de Dénombrement de 1891</u>. Paris: 1894.

_____: <u>Territoire et Population</u>. Paris: 1837.

_____: <u>Statistique agricole de la france...Résultats généraux de l'enquête décennale de 1840-1842</u>.

Freedman, Ronald.: Norms for Family Size in Underdeveloped Areas. <u>Proceedings of the Royal Society</u>. B., 1959:220, 1963.

Friedlander, D.: Demographic Responses and Population Change. <u>Demography</u>. 6:359 (Nov), 1969.

Gille, Bertrand.: <u>Les sources statistiques de l'histoire de france</u>. Paris: Librairie Minard, 1964.

Goreux, Louis.: <u>Agricultural Productivity and Economic Development in France, 1852-1950</u>. Michigan: Ann Arbor Microfilms.

Henry, Louis.: The Population of France in the Eighteenth Century, in Glass, D. V. and Eversley, D. E. C.: Population in History. London: Edward Arnold, 1965.

Henry, L., and Gautier, E.: La population de Crulai, paroisse Normande. Paris: 1958.

Hoffman, George Walter (ed).: Geography of Europe. London: Methuen, 1961.

Kindleberger, Charles P.: Economic Growth in France and Britain 1851-1950. New York: Simon and Schuster, 1964.

Lachiver, M.: La population de Meulan de xviie au xixe siècle. Paris: S. E. V. P. E. N., 1969.

Landry, A.: La révolution démographique. Études et essais sur les problèmes de la population. Paris: 1934.

Leroy-Beaulieu, P.: La question de la population. Paris: Felix Alcan, 1913.

Levasseur, E.: La population francaise. Vol. I-III. Paris: 1889-92.

Mounier, L.: De l'agriculture en france. Paris: Guillaumin, 1846.

Pautard, Jean.: Les disparites régionales dans la croissance de l'agriculture francaise. Paris: Gauthier-Villars, 1965.

Perroux, Francois.: Prise de vues sur la croissance de l'economie francaise, 1780-1950, in National Bureau of Economic Research.: Studies in Income and Wealth, v. V. Princeton: Princeton University Press, 1955.

Sauvy, A.: Théorie générale de la population. Paris: 1952.

Sée, Henri.: La vie économique de la france sous la monarchie censitaire 1815-1848. Paris: F. Alcan, 1927.

Singer, Charles, et. al. (eds).: A History of Technology, v. III. Oxford: Oxford University Press, 1957.

Slicher Van Bath, B. H.: The Agrarian History of Western Europe A. D. 500-1850. London: St. Martin's Press, 1963.

Spengler, J.: <u>France Faces Depopulation</u>. Durham, N. C.: 1938.

Toutain, J.-C.: <u>Le produit de l'agriculture francaise de 1700 à 1958</u> (in Cahiers de l'Institut de Science Économique Appliqué). Paris: I. S. E. A., 1961.

United Nations.: <u>Determinants and Consequences of Population Trends</u>. New York: 1953.

Van de Walle, E.: Demographic Transition in France? (mimeo).

_____: Marriage and Marital Fertility, in <u>Daedalus</u>. 97:486-501 (Spring), 1968.

Wright, Gordon.: <u>Rural Revolution in France</u>. Stanford: Stanford University Press, 1964.

Yasuba, Y.: <u>Birth Rates of the White Population of the United States, 1800-1860</u>. Baltimore: Johns Hopkins University Press, 1962.

x

LIST OF TABLES

List of Tables (continued)

LIST OF ILLUSTRATIONS

PREFACE

The rapid growth in population since World War II in underdeveloped countries has created widespread concern that already precariously low living standards may be driven down to levels of mass-starvation. Pressure on governments to take action has given rise to "derived demand" for information from social scientists on population control. In attempting to deal with the "population explosion" we have become painfully aware of our ignorance about how population growth and economic well-being are interrelated.

The problems of studying economic-demographic interrelations are compounded in underdeveloped countries by the general scarcity of reliable statistical information. One possible alternative is to study the past experience of now-developed countries as they went through a period of rapid population growth. Several now-developed countries had established extensive statistical records by the time they underwent the demographic transition. Such countries have the further advantage of providing an opportunity to study the complete transition from high birth and death rates to low birth and death rates. Naturally, important differences between countries preclude any simplistic parallels. Yet, it is possible that a study of how population growth in developed countries has interacted both with economic and demographic change might provide insight into the variety of relationships that can be expected among economic and demographic variables.

While extensive statistical records exist covering the past economic and demographic experience of developed countries, the information is generally not in a form in which it can be readily exploited. This study develops crude estimates of regional agricultural outputs and inputs for nineteenth century France from a major data source which was previously unutilized. These economic estimates are combined with available, but underutilized, regional demographic data to test various hypotheses about economic-demographic interrelations.

Aside from any light that the French experience might shed on the plight of underdeveloped countries, there is some inherent interest in both the demographic and economic history of France. France is generally conceded to be an exception to most explanations of the demographic transition. She starts the demographic transition fully a century before most of the rest of Western Europe. And in France, the birth rate so closely parallels the death rate decline that the resulting rates of population growth are very low relative to the rest of Europe. And economically, the role that agriculture plays in the economic development of France is quite obscure.

If it is possible to develop a model of economic-demographic inter-relations which can account for the peculiar behavior of France, we may have achieved significant progress towards understanding any general mechanisms by which population growth interacts with economic and demographic change.

CHAPTER I

POPULATION TRENDS IN NINETEENTH CENTURY FRANCE

Introduction

This chapter describes the trends in population growth and its basic

components in France from the Napoleonic Wars through the end of the

nineteenth century. Population trends are analyzed in terms of their

underlying components, first for the nation as a whole and then for a

regional grouping based on the proportion of the population living from

agriculture, the existence of major urban centers, and the height of the

birth rate at the turn of the nineteenth century. Finally the conclusions

from the regional analysis are tested using departments. Generalizations

about the interrelations between components are examined as well as the

conclusions about the influence of major urban centers and percent of

agriculture.

After a discussion of the controversy surrounding demographic trends

in the eighteenth century, an overview is presented of French population

change and its components from the eighteenth century to the mid-

twentieth century. Following a closer look at population change in the

nineteenth century for both the nation and its broad geographical regions,

a regional classification scheme is chosen and population change in those

regions is compared to the national trends. This regional description sets

out the associations between the components of population growth and

1

both the existence of major urban centers and the proportion of the population living from agriculture. Then, neglecting these associations, the
interrelations between the components are examined to see how they build
up to determine population growth.

While the choice of temporal focus is largely determined by the timing
of events and availability of data in French agriculture, important con-
straints on the demographic data limit the extent of the time period covered
in this chapter. By the turn of the nineteenth century Napoleon had carried
out both the political and administrative reorganization of France. Departments were formed from the old feudal provinces in 1800, and have
persisted with nearly intact boundaries to the present day. Nationwide
statistics, employing the new departmental units, were gathered for the
first time, and the first truly nationwide census was published in 1801.
Some "censuses" that followed were no more than adjustments of former
censuses for intervening births and deaths. However, useable censuses
were taken in 1801, 1821, 1831, and at regular five year intervals starting in 1841. Starting in 1801 figures for births and deaths were collected
by mayors and transmitted annually to prefectures who drew up summary
tables for arrondissements and departments and sent those summaries on
to Paris.[1] For the years prior to 1800, demographic data are scattered,
sporadic, and of uncertain reliability. Thus, from the point of view of

---

[1]B. Gille, Les Sources Statistiques de L'Histoire de France (Paris:
1964), p. 154.

consistent empirical data, 1801 is a natural benchmark.

Some minor boundary changes took place in France in the course of the nineteenth century. The decision was made to exclude from the regional analysis those areas gained by or lost to France during this period because of the difficulties of finding comparable demographic and economic data for those areas in the other countries involved. Table I lists the departments excluded, the date and the nature of their change in status, and their area in hectares (1 h = about 2 1/2 acres).

TABLE I

Departments of France Excluded from Study

Department	Date and Change	Area
Alpes-Maritimes	formed in 1860	391,662
Meurthe	dissolved in 1871	609,004
Meurthe-et-Moselle	formed in 1871	523,234
Moselle	dissolved in 1871	536,889
Rhin-Bas	formed in 1871	455,344
Rhin-Haut	reduced in 1871	410,771
Savoie	formed in 1860	575,950
Savoie-Haute	formed in 1860	431,472
France	before 1860	53,028,463

Although data are occasionally available in political units other than departments, the decision was made to maintain the departments as the basic unit of observation throughout the study both because it is the only subnational unit for which all demographic and economic data are available and because it allows extensive cross-sectional analysis with up to 80 observations on each variable.

Demographic Developments before 1800

As might be expected when the data are such crude estimates from inaccurate sources, considerable controversy surrounds the eighteenth century population trends in France. For the purposes of this study, it is sufficient to know only the broadest outlines of the national trends in the rate of total increase (RTI) and its components -- the crude birth rate (BR) the crude death rate (DR), and the rate of natural increase (RNI), and the rate of residual net migration (RRNM). Yet even for such an elementary demographic picture, important areas of disagreement persist.

The two conflicting views presented here are the work of Bourgeois-Pichat, whose original article appeared in 1951, and of Louis Henry, who wrote ten years later. Both articles appear in a major collection of essays on historical demography, Population in History.[2] Bourgeois-Pichat assumes that the death rate remained constant from 1700 to 1770, and

---

[2]D. Glass and D. Eversley (ed.), Population in History (Alva, Great Britain, 1965): J. Bourgeois-Pichat, "The General Development of the Population of France since the Eighteenth Century," pp. 474-506; and L. Henry, "The Population of France in the Eighteenth Century," pp. 434-456.

that the rate of total increase maintained an annual rate of 4 per thousand,

implying (in the absence of any net migration) a birth rate steady at level

4 per thousand higher than the death rate[3] and a rate of population growth

of about .4% per annum. Then around 1770, he argues, both the birth rate

and the death began a long steady fall, with the birth rate falling at least

as soon and as fast as the death rate.[4] Thus, he implies that the onset

of the death rate decline in France was not accompanied by the sizeable

acceleration in population growth which characterized the first stage of

the demographic transition in many countries where the birth rate only fell

with a lag which created a bulge in the rate of natural increases.

Louis Henry argues[5] for a different picture of the death rate decline.

Asserting that both the scant empirical evidence and our knowledge of

medical practices cast doubt on the likelihood of any continuous mortality

decline, he posits rather that the lower death rate from 1750 to 1790 was

---

[3]J. Bourgeois-Pichat, Ibid., pp. 482-482.

[4]Ibid., p. 490.

[5]Much of his discussion is based on reconstructions from parish
registers in isolated villages. The 1958 study he did with E. Gautier, La
population de Crulai, paroisse Normande, is the largest and most in-
fluential of these. Several more such parish studies came out in the
1960's. One of the most recent is Marcel Lachiver, La population de
Meulan de xvii[e] au xix[e] siecle, 1969. In this rural village outside Paris,
Lachiver finds evidence of family limitation among married women over
age 20 perhaps as early as 1740. As with all such small-scale studies,
however, its conclusions can not be taken as more than suggestive until
combined with many more such studies.

due instead to the absence of extraordinary mortality -- plagues, famines, and epidemics -- which had frequented France before 1750.[6] While he agrees with Bourgeois-Pichat that the birth rate did not begin to fall before 1775, the interaction of Louis Henry's death rate and the birth rate provide a rather different picture of the rate of natural increase, and (again ignoring migration) of the rate of total increase. In this view, the death rate retained a lower level for at least 20 years before the birth rate began to respond. So he concludes that while population grew very little if any up to 1750, it probably grew at a considerably faster rate than Bourgeois-Pichat claims from 1750 to 1790: Henry feels the growth in population which Bourgeois-Pichat would have spread out over the entire century was confined almost entirely to the second half of the century.

Figure 1 presents an idealized interpretation of each view in terms of the components of the rate of total increase.

In spite of the differing interpretations of the demographic events of the eighteenth century in France, the conclusion is inevitable that by starting in 1815 this study is dealing with the later stages of the demographic transition in France. If accelerating population growth put pressure on agriculture, this study can not observe it at the national level because, as the next section indicates, the peak population growth occurs no later than the second decade of the nineteenth century. Naturally, regional

---

[6]L. Henry, op. cit., pp. 447-448.

Figure 1: Idealized Drawing of Population Change: 1700-1800

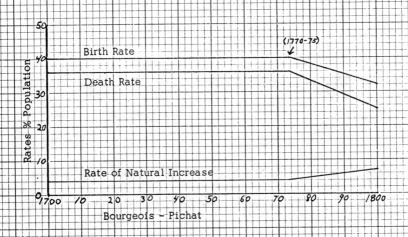

(1770-75)

Birth Rate

Death Rate

Rate of Natural Increase

Rates % Population

1700 10 20 30 40 50 60 70 80 90 1800

Bourgeois - Pichat

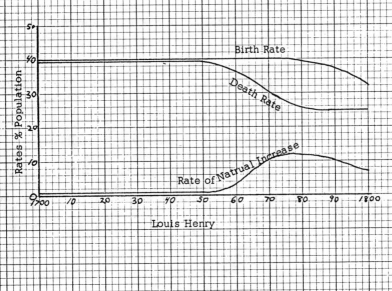

Birth Rate

Death Rate

Rate of Natural Increase

Rates % Population

1700 10 20 30 40 50 60 70 80 90 1800

Louis Henry

differentials in levels of population growth allow cross-sectional analysis, but the most striking economic effects of population growth can be expected to have occurred in the earlier period.

National Population Growth: 1800-1900

Figure 2 indicates that the declines of the death rate[7] in the late eighteenth century continue into the nineteenth century. Starting around 30 per thousand in 1800, the death rate falls to under 25 per thousand around 1840. The death rate then remains fairly stable until about 1890, with a bulge associated with the Franco-Prussian War. After 1890 it begins a steady but gradual decline to present day levels. It is possible that undernumeration of population in the first census and abnormally high deaths from the war activity lead to overstatement of the initial level of the death rate, hence to an overstatement of the decline in the first decades.

The birth rate appears to remain fairly stable at 32 per thousand up to 1820 while the death rate is still falling. From 1820 to 1850 the birth rate falls more rapidly than the death rate to a level of about 26 per thousand, where it remains until 1875 when it starts a fall to the death rate level of 23 per thousand in 1890. Thereafter, the birth rate closely parallels the death rate excepting a jump of 5 per thousand after World

---

[7]All rates per thousand of the population. Population base is geometric average of census populations; numerators are intercensal averages of annual data.

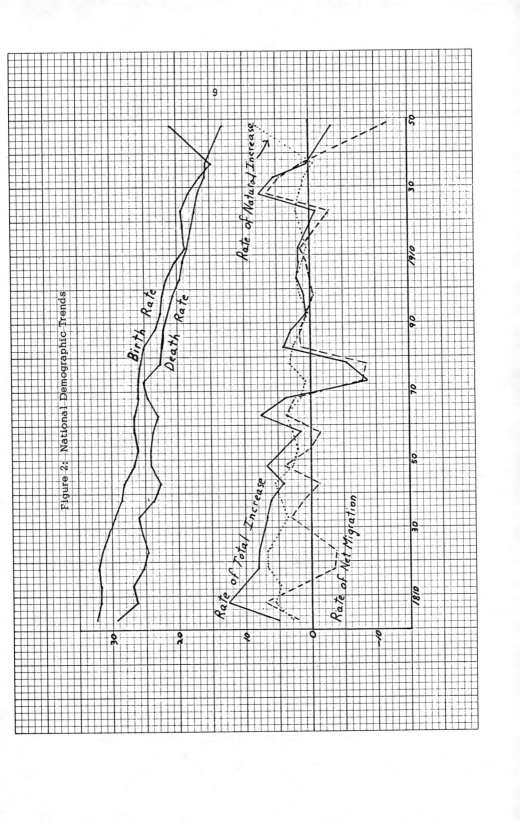

Figure 2: National Demographic Trends

War II.

The rate of natural increase, reflecting the difference between birth and death rates, rises from 3 per thousand around 1800 to a peak of nearly 7 per thousand in 1820. It shortly begins a slow decline to around 2 per thousand in 1890 where it remains until the post-World War II birth rate jump raises it to 6 or 7 per thousand. The movement in the rate of natural increase may reflect an earlier decline in the death rate and a lag in the birth rate decline, followed by a period when the birth rate catches up with the death rate. After 1850, the situation is remarkably stable through the 1930's with both birth and death rates edging down slowly and maintaining the rate of natural increase at a very low and stable level.

The rate of residual net migration, calculated as the difference between the rate of total increase and the rate of natural increase, is negligible for most of the nineteenth century. Some immigration is observed in the 1850's with the emigration associated with the Franco-Prussian War balancing it out. The apparent immigration in the first decade probably represents in part the underregistration in the first census. The lack of significant migration in the nineteenth century lends credence to the assumption that migration can be ignored in calculating the source of population change in the eighteenth century.

Because of the lack of significant net migration, net population increase follows very closely the pattern set by the rate of natural increase. The rate of total increase declines throughout most of the nineteenth century from a level of well under 10 per thousand in the first two decades to 1 or 2 per thousand by the last decade.

The overall national demographic picture for the nineteenth century includes a death rate starting at an already low level and dropping to a lower stable level around 1840. The birth rate falls steadily from 1820 to 1850, levels off to 1875, and then falls and catches up with the death rate in 1890. The rate of natural increase either starts down from its previous peak or reaches its peak in 1820, and falls sporadically to 2 per thousand in 1890. The rate of residual net migration is inconsequential. And the rate of total increase follows very closely the pattern of the rate of natural increase.

Put in broader perspective, population is stable because birth and death rates are nearly equal in the first half of the eighteenth century. Population growth starts in 1750 or 1775 depending on how one times the death rate decline. Population growth peaks in the 1770's or 1820 depending on whether the death rate reaches its lower level around 1775 or early in the nineteenth century. The birth rate decline begins no earlier than 1775. The growth in population declines from either 1775 or 1820, to 1890 depending on the timing of the mortality decline. And population is once again stable after 1890 as the further death rate decline is very closely matched by the birth rate, and net migration remains minimal. In the context of the two and one-half centuries from 1700 to 1950, the experience of the nineteenth century represents either the peak and then the

decline of population growth or the latter stages of the decline in population growth. Whichever characterization is accurate, this study, by
starting in 1815, must miss the buildup of population growth and the
events which lead to the onset of the birthrate decline. Still, it is
possible that there is enough regional variation in the timing of the demographic transition to allow some observation of the earlier stages of
demographic development in at least some parts of France. It is with this
general question that the rest of the chapter is concerned.

The Choice of Regional Units

The obvious starting place in choosing regions is to divide up the
country on a purely geographical basis. Table II gives the components
of the rate of total increase for 9 official geographical regions of France
and for the country as a whole. Each component is calculated for two
periods: period 1 from 1821-1846; and period 2 from 1846-1872. The
change in the level between period 1 and period 2 is also given for each
component as a measure of its trend. While some regional differences do
appear in levels and in trends, the overall conclusion must be that the
national levels and trends in the components of the rate of total increase
are replicated on a rather disaggregated level.

This conclusion is brought out even more clearly by Table III which
presents some summary measures of dispersion for each component. Coefficients of variation (standard deviation/mean) are very low for both
birth and death rates. While the coefficient of variation is less

TABLE II

Components of Rate of Total Increase by Geographical Area

Period 1: 1821-1846

Region	BR	DR	RNI	RNM	RTI
NW	27.09	22.93	4.160	-1.460	2.700
N	26.19	23.36	2.830	.640	3.470
NE	28.28	21.64	6.640	- .930	5.710
W	27.80	22.21	5.590	.090	5.680
C	29.12	23.88	5.240	- .620	4.620
E	28.90	24.02	4.880	-1.670	3.210
SW	26.09	22.54	3.550	- .270	3.290
S	29.09	23.43	5.660	-2.300	3.360
SE	31.48	25.09	6.390	-1.880	4.510

Period 2: 1846-1872

Region	BR	DR	RNI	RNM	RTI
NW	25.49	23.71	1.770	-2.780	-1.010
N	23.12	23.65	- .530	- .150	- .670
NE	24.17	22.08	2.090	-3.230	-1.140
W	25.98	21.59	4.390	- .700	3.690
C	25.10	22.25	2.850	-2.670	.180
E	25.22	24.17	1.060	-2.990	-1.930
SW	23.92	22.58	1.330	-2.800	-1.470
S	27.98	24.58	3.400	-4.010	- .610
SE	29.27	26.08	3.180	-3.820	- .640

Change from Period 1 to Period 2

Region	BR	DR	RNI	RNM	RTI
NW	-1.60	.7800	-2.390	-1.320	-1.690
N	-3.07	.2900	-3.360	- .790	-4.140
NE	-4.11	.4400	-4.550	-2.300	-6.850
W	-1.82	- .6200	-1.200	- .790	-1.990
C	-4.02	-1.630	-3.390	-2.050	-4.440
E	-3.68	.1500	-3.820	-1.320	-5.140
SW	-2.17	.0400	-2.220	-2.530	-4.760
S	-1.11	1.150	-2.260	-1.710	-3.970
SE	-2.22	.9900	-3.210	-1.940	-5.150

TABLE III

Summary Measures for Geographical Components
of Rate of Total Increase

(for Period 1, Period 2, and Change between Periods)

Component	low	high	mean	standard deviation	coefficient of variation
BR_1	26.09	31.48	28.226	1.6872	.06
BR_2	23.12	29.27	25.583	1.9589	.08
CBR	− 4.11	− 1.11	− 2.6444	1.1081	−−
DR_1	21.64	25.09	23.233	1.0426	.04
DR_2	21.59	26.08	23.409	1.4291	.06
CDR	− 1.63	1.15	.1766	.86408	−−
RNI_1	2.83	6.64	4.9933	1.2744	−−
RNI_2	− 0.53	4.39	2.1711	1.4713	−−
CRNI	− 4.55	− 1.20	−2.9333	1.0080	−−
RNM_1	− 2.30	.640	− .93333	.97754	−−
RNM_2	− 4.01	− .150	−2.5722	1.3090	−−
CRNM	− 2.53	− .790	−1.6388	.62654	−−
RTI_1	2.70	5.710	4.0611	1.1105	−−
RTI_2	− 1.93	3.690	− .39999	1.6448	−−
CRTI	− 6.85	− 1.690	−4.2366	1.5972	−−

meaningful when the mean is near zero or negative, the standard deviations
are still small and suggest relatively little dispersion for the other components.

Closer inspection of Table II raises the suspicion that these geographical units may hide more important differences in demographic behavior. The North region generally has the lowest birth rates and rates of
natural increase, and the highest rates of in-migration. The North

14

ontains Paris, the largest city in France, where high in-migration would
e expected. The southern regions seem to have somewhat more out-
igration than the northern regions. The southern regions are more
eavily agricultural and with percent of agriculture declining nationally,
ut-migration would be expected in the absence of significant non-agri-
ultural opportunities. These observations suggest that a regional class-
fication which groups departments by their degree of agriculture and
eparates out the largest cities might uncover differences in the com-
onents of total increase which are obscured by the geographical classifi-
ation. Such a classification scheme would be useful in uncovering
emographic factors in agricultural development, where large cities are
iappropriate to the analysis and where the degree of agriculture may be
n important variable.

Another approach might be to distinguish cultural, ethnic, or religious
roups in the nation. However, attempts to classify by such categories
rove no more successful in revealing differences than do the geographical
reakdown. In Hoffman, Geography of Europe, it is argued that France is
otable for its unity, not diversity. He argues that the early establish-
ient and continuation of a single national language is indicative of that
nity; further, he feels that the ideals of the French Revolution provided
n additional unifying influence. He concludes that "...there is no

regional concentration of any one class or group."[8]

The approach adopted here builds on the observed differences in the geographical regions, isolating some other interesting differences as well. The classification adopted is effectively three-way, based a) on the percentage of the population living in an urban (2,000 or more population in a town) setting; b) the proportion of the population living from agriculture; and c) the height of the birth rate in 1801. Table IV sets forth the regions and their predominant characteristics.

TABLE IV

Regional Classification

Region	% Urban	% Agriculture	Initial Birth Rate
1	High	----	----
2	Medium	----	----
3A	Low	Low	Low
3B	Low	Low	High
4A	Low	Medium	Low
4B	Low	Medium	High
5A	Low	High	Low
5B	Low	High	High

The regions are formed by aggregating departmental data. For example region 3A is the sum of the departments having a low enough proportion of their population living in cities and living from agriculture, and having a low enough birth rate in 1801. The population of region 3A is the sum of the populations of those departments. Thus the birth rate at any time for

---

[8]Hoffman, Geography of Europe (London: Methuen, 1961), p. 300.

egion 3A is the average of the birth rates of those departments weighted
by their populations.

The urban classification serves the function of separating Paris
(region 1) and Marseille and Lyon (region 2) from the rest of the country,
although the data actually refer to the departments of Seine, Bouches-du-
Rhone and Rhone, respectively, in which those cities are located. Outside the departments with the three largest cities, three levels of agriculture are distinguished: 23% to 50%, 50% to 65%, and 65% to 80%. (While
this classification is based on departmental data for 1891, the rank order-
ing of departments is essentially unchanged throughout the century,
although the absolute levels would be higher earlier in the century.)[9]
And again for all lower % urban departments, the departments are divided
on the basis of their birth rate in 1801: 24 to 33 per thousand, and 33 to
45 per thousand. It should be noted that the classification by % agriculture can be thought of as a crude geographical classification as well,
with low % agriculture in the North, and high % agriculture in the South.
Figure 3 provides a map showing the geographical distribution of the
regions.

Table V presents components of the rate of total increase for this
regional classification and for the nation as a whole. While national
levels and trends are roughly replicated by the regions, there is

---

[9]The correlation coefficient between % agriculture and 1891 and an
official government estimate of % rural for 1831 is .48.

Location of Regions by % Agriculture and Birth Rates
1801-1805

oticeably more regional variation than the geographical classification

showed in Table II. The greater dispersion under this regional classifica-

on is brought out more clearly by comparing Table VI and Table III. These

bles present measures to dispersion of the components for the three-way

assification and the geographical classification respectively. Regional

fferentials, especially in net migration, are brought out much more

early by the three-way classification.

egional Differences from the National Pattern

Figure 4 presents death rates for the various regions. National

uctuations are replicated by the regions throughout the period, while the

tional trend is a composite of regional trends with differing rates of

aange in the beginning of the period. By about 1890 the regional trends

ave largely converged on the national trend.

Paris or region 1 starts out with the highest death rate (37 per

ousand), continues with the highest death rate until 1880, then ends

ith the lowest death rate (17 per thousand). Marseille and Lyon or

gion 2 also start out with a higher death rate than any other region but

gion 1, but the death rate remains high throughout so by the end of the

eriod region 2 has the highest death rate. Through most of the period,

en, it is the major urban centers which have the highest death rate.

When the major urban centers are excluded, regional death rates

uster very closely around the national rate and replicate in striking de-

il the national pattern.

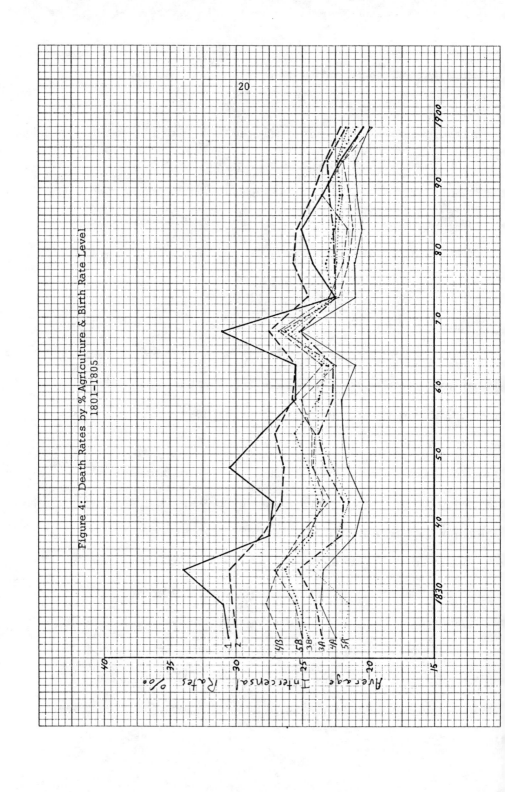

Figure 4: Death Rates by % Agriculture & Birth Rate Level
1801-1805

TABLE V

Components of Rate of Total Increase by 3-Way Classification

(% Urban, % Agriculture, Initial Birth Rate)

Period 1: 1821-1846

Region	BR	DR	RNI	RNM	RTI
Seine	32.96	30.11	2.85	15.35	18.21
Lyon & Marseille	32.87	28.60	4.27	7.49	11.76
Low Ag & Low BR	26.57	23.35	3.22	.76	3.98
Low Ag & Hi BR	30.97	24.86	6.11	.80	6.91
Med Ag & Low BR	26.13	22.11	4.02	- .16	3.86
Med Ag & Hi BR	30.86	25.62	5.24	.24	5.48
Hi Ag & Low BR	28.20	22.36	5.84	- 2.12	3.72
Hi Ag & Hi BR	29.87	25.00	4.87	- 1.20	3.67

Period 2: 1846-1872

Region	BR	DR	RNI	RNM	RTI
Seine	29.64	27.21	2.43	17.01	19.44
Lyon & Marseille	28.09	26.12	1.97	7.40	9.37
Low Ag & Low BR	24.08	23.37	.71	.66	1.37
Low Ag & Hi BR	28.41	24.35	4.06	- .65	3.41
Med Ag & Low BR	23.54	22.12	1.42	- 1.28	.14
Med Ag & Hi BR	27.58	24.18	3.40	- 1.80	1.60
Hi Ag & Low BR	26.55	23.62	2.93	- 3.90	- .97
Hi Ag & Hi BR	27.13	24.54	2.59	- 3.12	- .53

Change from Period 1 to Period 2

Region	BR	DR	RNI	RNM	RTI
Seine	-3.32	-2.90	- .42	1.66	1.23
Lyon & Marseille	-4.78	-2.48	-2.30	- .09	-2.39
Low Ag & Low BR	-2.49	- .02	-2.51	- .10	-2.61
Low Ag & Hi BR	-2.56	- .51	-2.05	-1.45	-3.50
Med Ag & Low BR	-2.59	.01	-2.60	-1.12	-3.72
Med Ag & Hi BR	-3.28	-1.44	-1.84	-2.04	-3.88
Hi Ag & Low BR	-1.65	1.26	-2.91	-1.78	-4.69
Hi Ag & Hi BR	-2.74	- .46	-2.28	-1.92	-4.20

TABLE VI

Summary Measures for 3-Way Classification of
Components of Rate of Total Increase

(for Period 1, Period 2, and Change between Periods)

Component	low	high	mean	standard deviation	coefficient of variation
BR_1	26.13	32.96	29.803	2.6286	.09
BR_2	23.54	29.64	26.877	2.1071	.08
CBR	- 4.78	- 1.65	- 2.9262	.91163	--
DR_1	22.11	30.11	25.251	2.8539	.11
DR_2	22.12	27.21	24.438	1.5938	.07
CDR	- 2.90	1.26	- .81749	1.3808	--
RNI_1	2.85	6.11	4.5524	1.1768	--
RNI_2	.71	4.06	2.4387	1.0732	--
CRNI	- 2.91	- .42	- 2.1137	.75947	--
RNM_1	- 2.12	15.35	2.6449	5.8917	--
RNM_2	- 3.90	17.01	1.7899	7.0624	--
CRNM	- 2.04	1.66	- .85499	1.2704	--
RTI_1	3.67	18.21	7.1987	5.2256	--
RTI_2	- .97	19.44	4.2287	6.9688	--
CRTI	- 4.69	1.23	- 2.9699	1.8612	--

High birth rate regions (B classification) all have death rates above

the national average and low birth rate regions (A classification) all have

death rates below the national average until after 1870. This observed

regional association between birth rate levels and death rate levels

suggests the hypothesis that birth rates may be responding to changes in

the death rate. This association is tested more directly at the end of the

chapter. Presumably the divergence from this pattern of association after

1870 implies that the birth rate classification begins to lose its validity, while it seems to hold well until then.

The tendency for the death rate for region 5A to rise for much of the nineteenth century may represent undernumeration at the beginning of the period. The departments in this region are found in the Massiff Centrale and the Pyrennees and are probably the most "backward" area of France.

There seems to be no systematic variation in death rates by % agriculture.

Figure 5 presents the regional birth rate trends.

Both national trends and fluctuations are reflected in the regional birth rate graphs, with the primary difference being the levels. Although there is more overall regional fluctuation than there is for the death rate, there is less when regions 1 and 2 (the major urban centers) are excluded.

Regions 1 and 2 have higher birth rates than the rest of the country until 1860, but they fall faster so that, by 1911, they have the lowest rates. Unlike the case of the death rate, birth rate patterns for regions 1 and 2 are nearly identical and remain so throughout the period. The major urban centers, then, have the highest mortality levels but they are balanced by the highest fertility,[10] so the relative levels of their rates of natural increase are not obvious a priori.

---

[10]This finding of higher fertility rates in large urban areas runs counter to the expectations from the literature on fertility and urbanization (see U. N., Determinants and Consequences, p. 78). It is possible the higher urban birth rate is due to differences in age-structure.

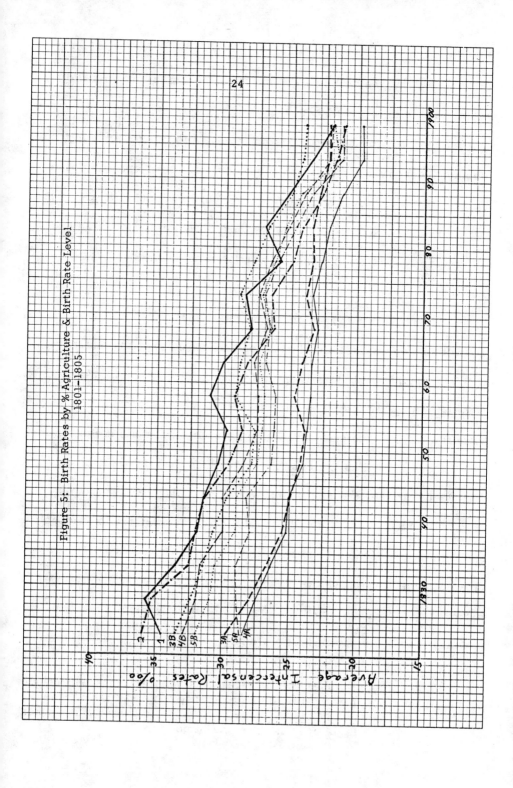

Figure 5: Birth Rates by % Agriculture & Birth Rate Level
1801-1805

Initially, there is more compact clustering of birth rates by the birth rate classification than there was for death rates, as would be expected from the definition of the classification. It seems from the dissipation of clustering after 1885 that the classification using the birth rate level at the beginning of the period has little significance in the last 25 years of the period.

The noteable exception to the regional clustering is again region 5A, where the failure of the birth rate to fall until the 1870's again suggests undernumeration for much of the nineteenth century.

There seems to be no systematic variation in birth rates by % agriculture.

Figure 6 presents the regional graphs for the rate of natural increase.

While there is a tendency for the regional trends and fluctuations in the rate of natural increase to follow the national pattern, the tendency is slightly less pronounced than in the case of either birth rates or death rates. Such a result is expected as the rate of natural increase is calculated as the difference between the birth rate and the death rate, picking up the deviations of each from the national trend. While some deviations may cancel each other, others can be expected to magnify each other.

When major urban centers are excluded, however, there is even more regional clustering around the national level than there is for birth or death rates.

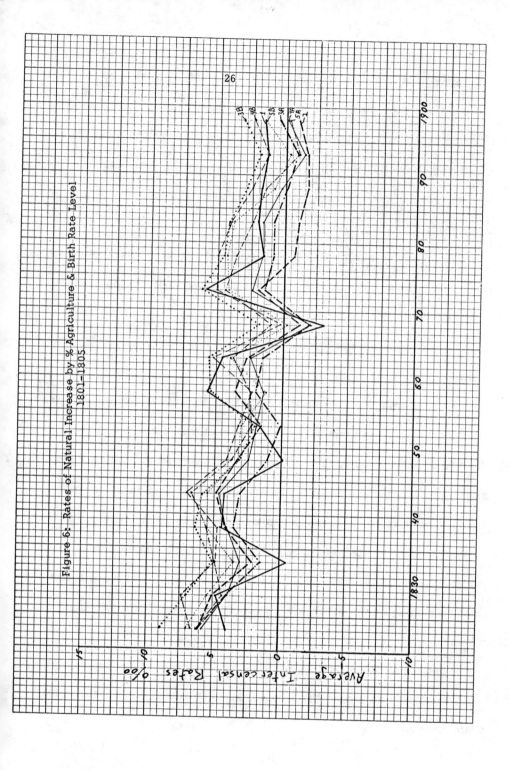

Figure 6: Rates of Natural Increase by % Agriculture & Birth Rate Level
1801-1805

While regional deviations in both trends and fluctuations are greater

the rate of natural increase than for either birth rates or death rates,

regional variations in levels is less for the rate of natural increase

n for either birth or death rates. We may hypothesize that the birth

responds with quite uniform sensitivity to the death rate level. This

ervation becomes quite important in assessing the interrelations

lysis later in the study where the lack of wide cross-sectional varia-

in the rate of natural increase makes it difficult to discern its impact

other variables.

The major urban centers -- regions 1 and 2 -- and especially Paris

w a marked tendency to maintain rates of natural increase lower than

national average. As their death rates and birth rates are both above

national average, it is apparent that their high mortality outweighs

r high fertility.

There is a pronounced tendency for regions with low initial birth rates

lassification) to have low rates of natural increase, and high initial

h rate regions (B classification) to have high rates of natural increase.

apparent association between birth rate level and the level of the

of natural increase will be examined at the end of the chapter.

As might be expected, region 5A which had a higher birth rate than

licted also has a higher rate of natural increase.

On the other hand, there still seems to be no systematic variation by

griculture.

Figure 7 gives the regional rates of residual net migration.

The rate of net migration for a region is calculated as the difference between its rate of total increase and natural increase.

What little national migration does occur probably emanates more from major urban centers than from rural areas.[11] Consequently, rates of residual net migration for regions 3, 4, and 5 can be interpreted as inter-regional rates, eliminating the issue of whether out-migration from one region represents in-migration in other regions or inter-country migration as well.

Regional variations in net migration are very impressive. Although some strong patterns in fluctuations emerge, observable countercyclical fluctuations also seem to exist.

Throughout the century, the figure is dominated by fluctuations in net migration for major urban centers. Until the 1870's or even 1880's (when the significance of the classification scheme begins to break down, any-way) regions 1 and 2 completely dominate the in-migration pattern. While Paris exhibits significantly higher levels of in-migration than Lyon and Marseille, the difference between major urban centers is minor compared to the differences between the major urban centers and the rest of France. For migration patterns, at least, it seems that the important distinction is not between Paris and the rest of France as is traditional, but between the

---

[11]United Nations, <u>Determinants and Consequences of Population Trends</u> (New York, 1953), p. 112.

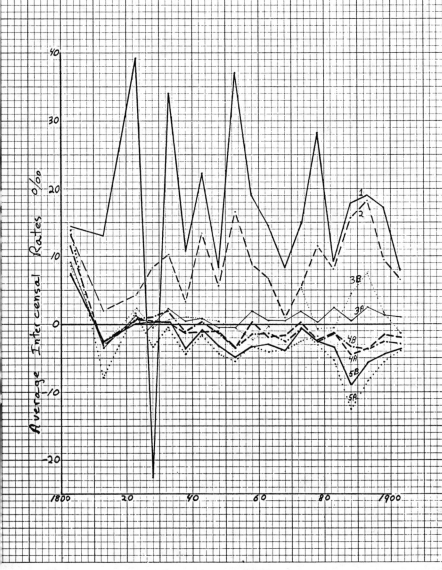

Figure 7

Rates of Residual Net Migration by % Agriculture and
Birth Rate Level, 1801-1805

major urban centers and the rest of France.[12] Experimentation with the

departments containing the next largest cities in France indicates that

this urban pattern very quickly approaches the non-urban pattern as the

size of cities declines.

When the major urban centers are excluded, most of the regional

variation is eliminated. While for the period as a whole there is more

variation in the rate of net migration than in the other components, there

is probably less variation at the beginning of the period than at the end.

The regional variation increases throughout the century.

Unlike the other components of the rate of total increase, the rates

of residual net migration show systematic regional variation by % agricul-

ture. The more agricultural a region, the lower the rate of residual net

migration. This relationship seems very strong, indeed. While it seems

more pronounced later in the period, that is probably due to the fanning

out of the regional rates; inter-regional migration becomes more pronounce

as the century progresses.

The regional differentials by the birthrate classification give rise to

two interesting conclusions. First, there seems to be no systematic

variation by initial birth rate level. Second, the two samples (classifica-

tions A and B) for each level of % agriculture give almost identical results

The first conclusion indicates that other than the impact of major urban

---

[12]"The only distinction that can and should be made is between Paris
and the rest of France." Hoffmann, op. cit., p. 300.

centers, natural increase and migration are determined by different factors -- birth and death rates, and % agriculture respectively. The second conclusion suggests that the influence of % agriculture on net migration is not only strong but uniform as well.

While in-migration is dominated by the major urban centers, two other regions maintain levels of in-migration which are low but still consistent. These are regions 3A and 3B, both low % agriculture regions. As the regions of medium % agriculture maintain low but fairly consistent levels of out-migration, the inference is that the cut-off level is around 50% agriculture or the highest % agriculture included in regions 3; departments with less than 50% of their population living from agriculture can be expected to have in-migration; and departments with more than 50% agriculture should have out-migration.

While the pattern is by no means obvious, there does seem to be some expected tendency for regions of high in-migration to have fluctuations counter to those for high out-migration.

The break in the trend for region 3B between 1866 and 1876 is due to boundary changes.

Figure 8 presents the regional rates of total increase.

Because the rate of total increase is the sum of the rates of natural increase and residual net migration, the trends and fluctuations of each component must be represented in the resulting population growth. The relative importance of natural increase and net migration is not so readily

Figure 8

Rates of Total Increase by % Agriculture and
Birth Rate Level, 1801-1805

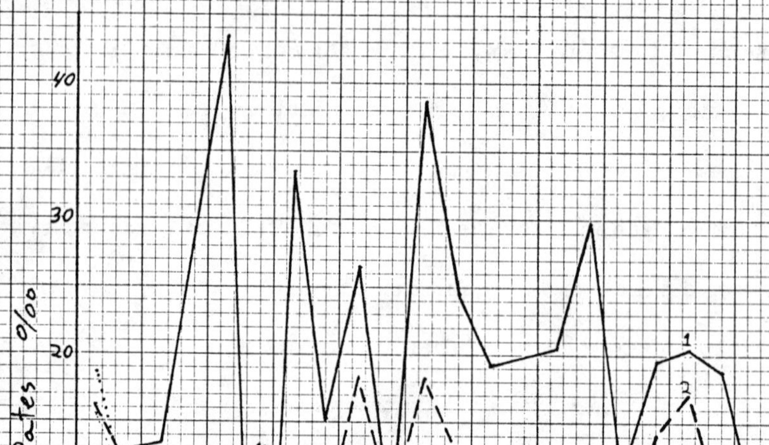

apparent, however. Their relative impact on total increase is discussed in the next section.

The rate of total increase for the major urban centers is very high and widely fluctuating, with the level for Paris higher and more volatile than for Marseille and Lyon. Clearly, here the rate of residual net migration completely dominates the rate of total increase, with the lower than average rate of natural increase doing little more than dampening slightly the basic migration trend.

Excluding the major urban centers, there is surprisingly little regional variation from the national pattern, either in trend, level, or fluctuation, for the period up to 1880.

Within the narrow regional differentials, some systematic variation by both % agriculture (from the net migration component of total increase) and initial birth rate (from the natural increase component) is evident. The variation by % agriculture is more pronounced, indicating that the net migration component may be relatively more important even for the non-urban regions.

While interesting regional differences appear in the components of the rate of total increase from Figures 4 to 9, much of those differences seem to be attributable to major urban centers. The major urban centers have higher birth rates, death rates, and rates of in-migration, and lower rates of natural increase. Because the rates of in-migration are so strikingly different from the rest of the nation, their rates of total increase are strikingly higher than the rest of France.

When major urban centers are excluded, the overwhelming conclusion must be that the national patterns for the components of the rate of total increase are very closely replicated for the regions of France. This replication holds whether we refer to levels, trends, or fluctuations around a trend. The greatest regional differences appear in the levels of net migration, where there is a pronounced tendency for more agricultural regions to have more out-migration. The regional uniformity of demographic trends makes it meaningful to discuss national demographic developments. On the other hand, it makes it difficult to test out the impact of demographic developments by observing regional differentials.

Departmental Analysis

In this section, observations made at the regional level are tested more rigorously at the departmental level by regression analysis. The observations on major urban centers are not dealt with here because there are too few centers to use regression techniques.

The first part of this section is concerned with the association of the different components with % agriculture. We observed that no systematic relationship seemed to exist between birth rates, death rates, or rates of natural increase and % agriculture, while both rates of net migration and rates of total increase seemed to be inversely associated with % agriculture.

Table VII presents the results of regressing each of the components of the rate of total increase against % agriculture for both periods (1821-1846 and 1846-1872). These results simply confirm the observations made on the regional level. % agriculture is strongly associated with the level of the rate of net migration, and very significantly but less strongly associated with the level of the rate of total increase.

A separate set of observations made on the regional level concerned the interrelationships between the components of the rate of total increase. Birth rates and death rates seemed strongly related. Birth rates and rates of natural increase also seemed associated. On the other hand, birth rates did not appear to be related to rates of net migration or rates of total increase. And rates of total increase seemed to reflect rates of both natural increase and net migration, but the impact of net migration rates seemed stronger.

Table VIII sets out the regression results for both periods for these interrelationships. The observation that birth rates and death rates are strongly associated is upheld. The high r^2 suggests the hypothesis that the death rate is the most important single influence on the birth rate. The strength of this association is remarkable: a change of 1.0 o/oo in the death rate can be expected to be accompanied by a change of 1.1 o/oo in the birth rate. This hypothesized "overreaction" of the birth rate to the death rate might be explained by the fact that declines in the death rate in the nineteenth century reflect primarily declines in infant mortality.

The regional analysis suggested a relationship between birth rates and rates of natural increase. Even if such an association exists, it is not clear if the relationship is direct, or works through a relationship between death rates and rates of natural increase. The regression results make it clear that the association is between birth rates and rates of natural increase, not between death rates and rates of natural increase. The importance of birth rates in 'explaining' rates of natural increase is as great as the importance of death rates in 'explaining' birth rates.

Some evidence exists for an association between rates of natural increase and net migration: the greater the natural increase the more out-migration. However, the evidence is mixed and the estimated relationship weaker than those discussed above. The association is significant in period 1 when the relationship between % agriculture and rate of net migration is weaker. It is possible that lack of variation in both variables, but especially in natural increase, obscures an existing relationship, especially in the presence of % agriculture which has such a strong impact on migration.

The results of the regressions of the rate of total increase with the rate of natural increase and the rate of net migration do not entirely fulfill the expectations formed from the regional analysis. As expected, both natural increase and net migration are associated with total increase, but natural increase turns out to be more important in explaining total increase.

TABLE VII

Regression on % Ag

Dependent Variable	Coefficient	Std. Error of Coeff.	Constant	t-ratio	Sig. Level	r^2
BR_1	0.0165	0.0319	27.6552	0.41	--	.0035
BR_2	0.0275	0.0326	24.1104	0.84	--	.0093
DR_1	-0.0029	0.0235	24.1187	0.12	--	.0002
DR_2	0.0119	0.0191	22.9191	0.62	--	.0050
RNI_1	0.0194	0.0188	3.5359	1.03	--	.0138
RNI_2	0.0204	0.0231	1.3148	0.88	--	.0101
RNM_1	-0.0751	0.0135	3.9900	5.56	.9995	.2890
RNM_2	-0.1077	0.0178	4.3694	6.03	.9995	.3230
RTI_1	-0.0568	0.0195	7.5845	2.91	.995	.1001
RTI_2	-0.0900	0.0275	5.4804	3.27	.995	.1234

78 observations

TABLE VIII

Dependent Variable	Independent Variable	Coeffi- cient	Coeff. of Std Error	Term Constant	t- ratio	Sig. Level	r^2
BR_1	DR_1	1.0957	.0918	2.2993	11.94	.9995	.65
BR_2	DR_2	1.1323	.1468	-1.0786	7.71	.9995	.44
RNI_1	BR_1	.4016	.0498	-6.8781	8.06	.9995	.46
RNI_2	BR_2	.5733	.0482	-12.2571	11.89	.9995	.65
RNI_1	DR_1	.092467	.091557	2.3759	1.01	---	.01
RNI_2	DR_2	.12254	.13869	-.463	0.88	---	.01
RNM_1	RNI_1	- .2830	.0914	1.2113	3.10	.99	.11
RNM_2	RNI_2	- .1942	.1045	-1.0075	1.86	.90	.04
RTI_1	RNI_1	.7239	.0928	1.1762	7.80	.9995	.44
RTI_2	RNI_2	.8430	.1074	-1.4519	7.85	.9995	.45
RTI_1	RNM_1	.61082	.12959	4.5544	4.71	.995	.23
RTI_2	RNM_2	.77754	.12686	1.7422	6.13	.9995	.33

This analysis concludes that several important inter-relationships
ist between the demographic magnitudes. Death rates are associated
th birth rates. Rates of natural increase are associated with birth rates.
tes of net migration may be inversely associated with rates of natural
crease. And rates of total increase are associated with rates of both
tural increase and net migration.

nclusions

The picture which emerges from this chapter is a country which is
mographically mature. The demographic transition started around
50 with a decline in the death rate. Depending on how one estimates
e timing of the birth rate decline, population growth reaches its peak
ound 1775 or 1820. While the nineteenth century is marked by impor-
nt declines in the death rate, the decline is remarkably uniform through-
it France. The response of the birth rate is both rapid and quite uniform
ross the country. Natural increase starts the nineteenth century at a
irly low level, and declines throughout the country. The variation in
e rate of natural increase within the country is even less than for birth
nd death rates. Outside of the largest cities, the rate of net migration
 fairly uniform by department, although it exhibits more regional varia-
ons than any other of the components of rate of total increase. What
gional migration there is seems to be primarily rural-urban migration.
he rate of total increase declines during the nineteenth century, and that

pattern of decline is replicated with some regional variation throughout the country.

Major urban areas seem to be the largest single source of national variation. They are associated with high birth and death rates, low rates of natural increase, high rates of in-migration, and high rates of total increase. Outside the major urban areas, there is an association between the proportion of the population living from agriculture and net migration: the more agricultural an area, the more the out-migration. There is also a weaker positive association between % agriculture and rate of total increase.

Significant interrelationships exist between various components of the rate of total increase. Birth and death rates are very strongly positively related, as are birth rates and rates of natural increase. Rates of natural increase and net migration may have some inverse relationship. And the rate of total increase is related positively to both rates of natural increase and net migration.

The regional classification developed in this chapter brings out almost all of the regional variation found in demographic behavior in nineteenth century France. If any of these demographic magnitudes have an impact on agricultural behavior, the relationship should emerge when the agricultural variables are calculated for these regions. However, the regional similarity of demographic behavior, which makes it meaningful to speak of the demographic development of France as a whole, makes it ifficult to test any conclusions drawn about the impact of that demo-

raphic development of observing regional differentials.

CHAPTER II

FRENCH AGRICULTURE IN THE NINETEENTH CENTURY

Introduction

This chapter describes the trends in agricultural production and its components in nineteenth century France. It analyzes the trends in output first by inputs and their productivity and then by type of output both for the nation as a whole and for a regional grouping based on the proportion of the population living from agriculture and the height of the birth rate in 1801. Finally the national trends in agriculture are compared to the literature on French agriculture in the nineteenth century.

The choice of 1815 as a starting point for the analysis is entirely determined by the availability of data. Prior to that date, annual agricultural data for the nation as a whole is not available for any crop, and other than occasional crude estimates by individual authors of the total value of French agricultural production, the only figures available are for isolated crops or head of cattle for a few years after 1800. After 1815, annual data on production, hectares planted, and yield is available for the roughly 86 departments of France for seven major cereals and potatoes. No further significant improvements in the data occur until the first agricultural census of 1840. The choice of 1900 as the terminal date for the study has motivation in the data as well as in the timing of the

velopments in agriculture and population: agricultural data on the

partmental level are phased out of the French statistical sources in the

st part of the nineteenth century and are completely eliminated in 1897.

Although data are occasionally available in political units other than

partments, the decision was made to maintain the department as the

sic unit of observation throughout the study both because it is the only

bnational unit for which all demographic and economic data are avail-

le and because it allows extensive cross-sectional analysis with up to

observations on each variable.

RT I. THE EMPIRICAL RECORD

National Patterns in Agriculture

The source of the data for the agricultural patterns analysed in this

ction is a volume by J. C. Toutain, Le produit de l'agriculture

ancaise de 1700 à 1958: II. - La Croissance[1] in the series Histoire

antitative de l'Économie francaise by the I.S.E.A. (L'Institute de

cience Économique Appliqueé). This series represents a major effort by

e I.S.E.A. to bring together all the empirical evidence possible on the

ench economy since 1700 into a unified body of data constituting the

st available national statistics on modern French economic history.

---

[1]J. C. Toutain, Le produit de l'agriculture francaise de 1700 à 1958:
. - La Croissance in Cahiers de L'Institute de Science Économique
ppliquee (Histoire Quantitative de L'Économie Francaise (2)): (I.S.E.A.:
aris), 1961.

While the series is far from complete, the volumes on agriculture have been finished since 1961. This source is the obvious starting point for any empirical discussion of national agricultural patterns in the nineteenth century.

Figures 1 and 2 present an overview of the major trends in French agriculture from 1775 to 1950.

The trend in total real agricultural production in Figure 1 can be split into four periods: 1775-1820, slow growth; 1820-1870, rapid growth; 1870-1890, stagnation; and 1890 on, moderate growth. Since population grows slowly and steadily from 1775 to 1850, then stagnates after 1850, per capita production is constant from 1775 to 1820 before growing rapidly to a peak in 1870. After stagnation to 1890, growth is resumed at a lower level until World War II.

Figure 2 shows the graphs for the trends in the inputs of land and labor and their average products for comparison with the trend in production.

Slow growth in the labor input and more rapid growth in the land input, with no productivity increase, account for the slow growth in production from 1775 to 1820.

The primary explanation for the rapid growth in production from 1820 to 1870 is rapid productivity increases: the labor input grows slowly and the land input has almost no growth to 1850, and both are fairly constant after 1850.

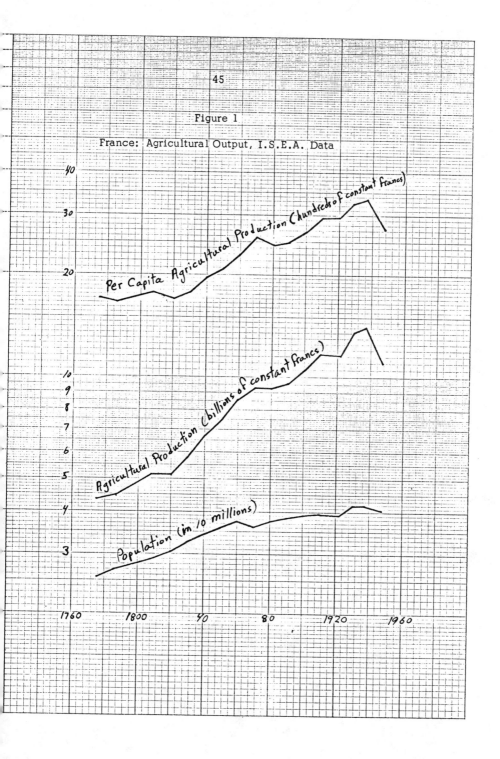

Figure 1

France: Agricultural Output, I.S.E.A. Data

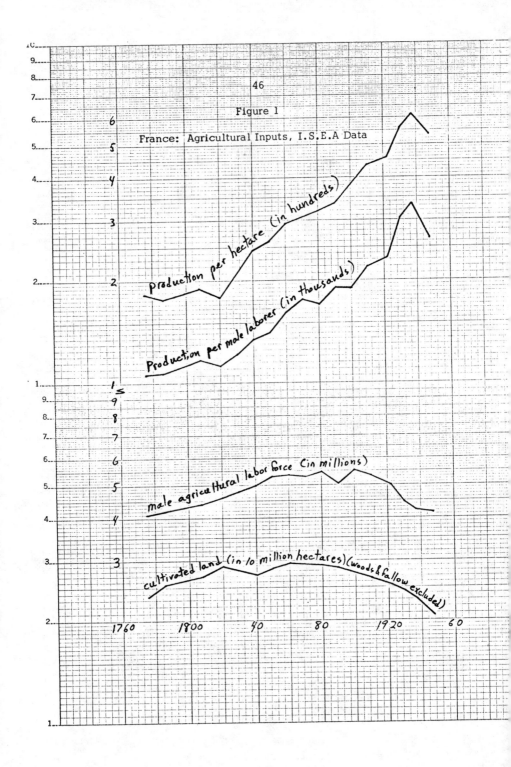

46

Figure 1

France: Agricultural Inputs, I.S.E.A Data

production per hectare (in hundreds)

Production per male laborer (in thousands)

male agricultural labor force (in millions)

cultivated land (in 10 million hectares)(woods & fallow excluded)

1760   1800   40   80   1920   60

From 1870 to 1890, the stagnation in production is accounted for by constant or slightly declining inputs of land and labor with modest productivity increases.

Despite accelerating declines in both land and labor inputs, productivity increases in both inputs, exceeding the rates of growth of the 1820-70 period after 1920, allow a moderate growth in production after 1890.

In general, while both inputs only grow slowly to the mid-nineteenth century and then decline, the land input stops growing and begins its decline earlier; thus, the ratio of labor to land inputs (the man/land ratio) rises very slowly throughout the nineteenth century.

The over-all picture that emerges from Figures 1 and 2 is of the most important growth in agriculture of the last two centuries occuring in the period from 1820 to 1870. While growth in land and labor inputs accounts for some of this rapid growth in production, the important sources of growth are the productivity increases in both land and labor.

The rest of this section focuses on the output components of total agricultural production, attempting to determine whether growth in agricultural production is concentrated in any one product or group of products.

Figure 3 shows total (feed and seed excluded; constant francs) and disposable vegetable and animal production in comparison to total agricultural production.

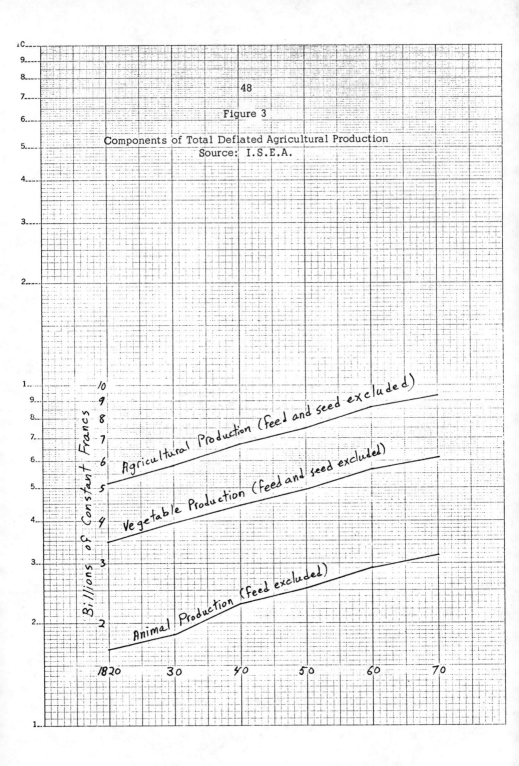

48

Figure 3

Components of Total Deflated Agricultural Production
Source: I.S.E.A.

Vegetable production is the largest proportion of total production (varying between 71% and 78% in the nineteenth century), and has virtually identical trends with total production until 1870 when it declines slightly instead of remaining constant. Animal production follows a roughly similar trend to vegetable production until 1870, but continues to grow at the same rate after 1870, providing a counterbalance to the decline in vegetable production. Up to 1870, when the period of rapid growth in which the study is interested ends, vegetable production is the most important component (76% to 78%) of total production, with which it maintains a virtually identical trend. While less important than vegetable production, animal production does exhibit similar rates of growth.

Figure 4 shows the important vegetable crops (feed included). While straw and root forage crops are produced in larger quantities than cereals (seed included), cereals dominate disposable vegetable crops, with only potatoes (seeds excluded) and wine in the same order of magnitude. Cereals (and straw) have trends nearly identical to total vegetable production. Forage crops grow faster, but do not receive coverage until 1840 or 1850 (with the first agricultural censuses); potatoes grow faster (with a major setback in 1846 from the potato bug); wine and cider grow lower and less evenly. In general for the period from 1820 to 1870, cereals dominate disposable vegetable production (varying between 33% and 40% of total vegetable production) and (with straw) replicate closely the trend in total vegetable production.

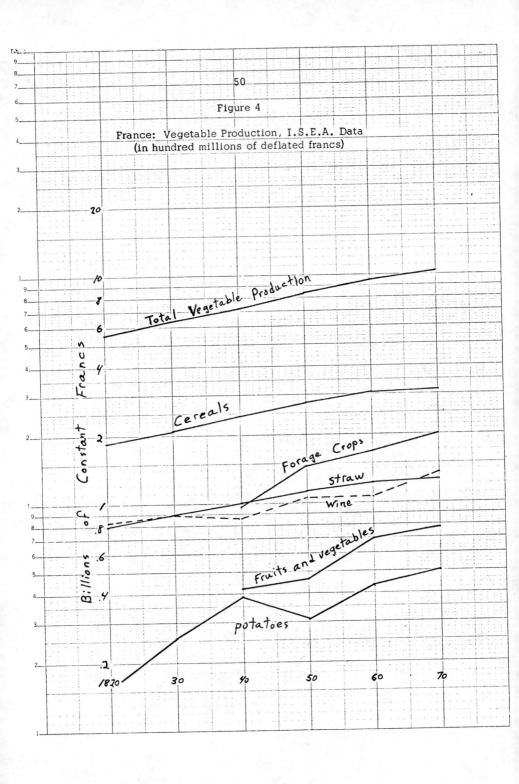

Figure 4

France: Vegetable Production, I.S.E.A. Data
(in hundred millions of deflated francs)

Figure 5 presents the quantities of the various cereal crops (seeds included).

While wheat is the most important cereal crop (varying from 37% to 46% of total cereal production, 1820-1870), three or even four cereals dominate the total. Of those, wheat and oats grow slightly faster than the total while barley grows only slightly and rye declines. Farmers seem to be phasing out both rye, and mixed wheat and rye after 1840. In general, all non-rye cereal crops share in the growth in output, with the two most important crops growing fastest, so that by 1870 wheat and oats account for 67% of the quantity of total cereal production.

Figure 6 gives the quantities produced of the major animal products.

Meat (29% to 48%), milk (35% to 18%), and butter and cheese (14% to 16%), which dominate animal production in value terms, all exhibit similar growth patterns to each other and to the trend for total animal production. Silk and wool follow quite different patterns from other animal products but represent a very small (2% to 5%, and 3% to 10%, respectively) proportion in value terms of total animal production. In general, all major animal products have remarkably similar trends.

The general picture which emerges of the trends in agricultural production during the period of rapid growth (1820-1870) is one of uniformity of growth in the major vegetable and animal crops. Vegetable crops dominate total agricultural production; disposable vegetable crops are dominated by cereals; and among cereals several crops -- wheat, oats

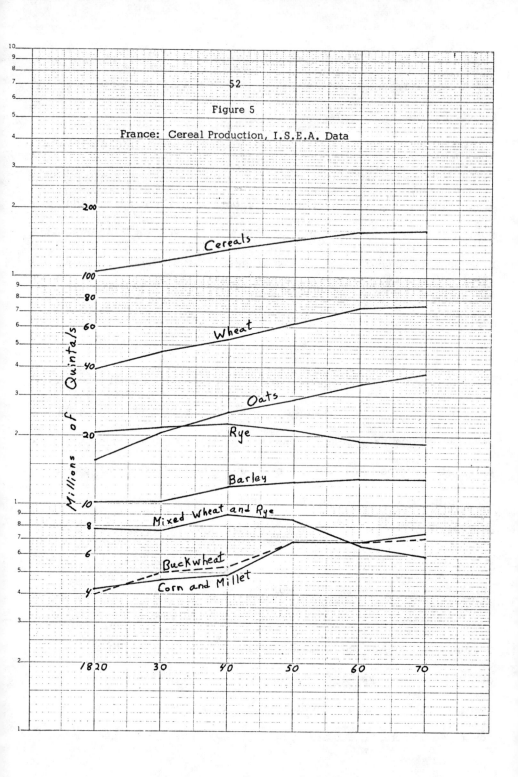

Figure 5

France: Cereal Production, I.S.E.A. Data

Cereals

Wheat

Oats

Rye

Barley

Mixed Wheat and Rye

Buckwheat

Corn and Millet

Millions of Quintals

200

100

80

60

40

20

10

8

6

4

1820   30   40   50   60   70

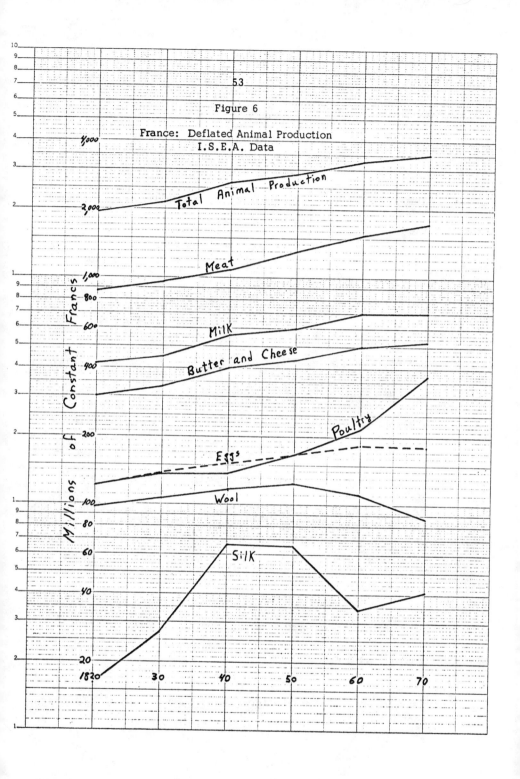

53

Figure 6

France: Deflated Animal Production
I.S.E.A. Data

rye and maybe barley -- predominate. Among the animal components of total production, meat, milk, and perhaps butter and cheese account for the largest proportions of total animal production in value terms. Cereals and animal products seem to characterize French agriculture in the nineteenth century, and they seem to share quite uniformly in the important growth in the period 1820 to 1870.

B. Development of Regional Indicators

While J. C. Toutain's I.S.E.A. study constitutes probably the best single body of national data on French agriculture, it contains no regional information. Besides the use of departmental data for regression analysis for 1860 at the earliest, little use seems to have been made of what departmental data are available in official government sources. In the absence of already processed regional data in secondary sources, the attempt must be made to use what official statistics are available.

With the publication by the Statistique Generale de la France in 1878 of Annuaire Statistique de la France,[2] annual departmental data on production, hectares, and yield are available from 1877 to 1897 for all major cereals, potatoes, industrial crops, forage crops, wine, cider, beer and occasionally other minor vegetable crops, with some variation in coverage over the twenty year period.

---

[2]Statistique Generale de la France, Annuaire Statistique de la France, 1878-present (Paris).

Prior to 1877, the most accessible regional information can be found in various agricultural censuses or _enquêtes_. Censuses are available for 1840, 1852, 1862, 1866, 1872, and 1876.[3] In addition to data on cereals and potatoes, they also have statistics on head of domestic animals, on natural and artificial meadows, and on fallow land. While these sources provide useful benchmarks for the last half of the period of rapid growth, they do not provide the desired insight into its first two decades.

From 1815, mayors reported each year the results of the harvest to the prefects, whose reports are generally well preserved in the departmental archives. Occasional obscure governmental publications contain this departmental data for some of the years before 1840, although little of it is available in this country. The Library of Congress, however, does have a (mis-catalogued) retrospective edition published by the Ministère de l'Agriculture,[4] which summarizes all the annual departmental data from 1815 to 1876 on production, hectares, and yield for the seven major cereals and potatoes. Although it is understandable in the light of the general unavailability of these departmental data that they have not been utilized in the United States, it is less clear why such an extensive data base has not been exploited in France.

---

[3]B. Gille, _Les Sources Statistiques de L'Histoire de France_ (Paris: 1964), pp. 196-200.

[4]France. Ministère de l'Agriculture, _Racoltes des Cereales et des Pommes de Terre_, 1815-1876 (Paris: 1913).

Apparently the reason for largely ignoring the non-census departmental

statistics for agriculture seems to have been their presumed unreliability.

In a volume assessing French statistical sources, Bertrand Gille writes of

these data (my translation):[5]

> The states of the harvest appear to have been better pre-
> served. They are available in quite large numbers in the
> departmental archives... There is little likelihood that the
> figures given by the prefects are exact. The prefects had
> absolutely no way of supervising the data furnished them
> by the mayors. These last, moreover, had no way in
> practice, before the completion of land surveys, to know the
> area cultivated, and thus, the product of the harvest.
> Moreau de Jonnes is of the opinion that one can place no
> confidence whatsoever in these figures, even for using them
> solely as gross indicators. These are the numbers which
> actually figure in the retrospective tables of the French
> General Statistics Office. It is best, no doubt, to pay
> absolutely no attention to them.

It is true that there are extensive errors in the data, many of them

typographical. A number were located in this study by internal checks

(production = hectares times yield) and by plotting every series against

time.

It is easy, however, to find fault with historical data: the difficulty

lies in assessing what maximum use can be made of the little information

available. Even crude data can be useful if only crude conclusions are

derived from it: certainly it is better to take into account what data

exists, however inaccurate, than to rely solely on nonquantitative

sources. Further, it can be argued that the unreliability of these data

---

[5]Gille, op. cit., p. 158.

can be over-estimated. The data do cover every department of France.
They were collected on an extremely disaggregated level, in close physical
proximity to the actual operations. As long as the errors are randomly
distributed, they should have some tendency to cancel each other when
aggregated into departments and especially when departments are aggregated into regions. Most importantly, while the figures may be poor
approximations to absolute levels they may reflect with much greater
accuracy rates of growth. For example, a mayor may seriously under-
estimate the number of hectares cultivated in his commune, and still have
a much better impression of the amount of change in area cultivated: even
if the levels are <u>consistently</u> wrong, the trends may be fairly accurate.

Some confidence can be placed in the data because the I.S.E.A.
study uses it, albeit on the national level, as one of its major sources.
When one checks for internal consistency between the yield levels from
the retrospective data, and the intensity of manure application, predominant farm animals, and the number of advanced farm machinery given
in the censuses from 1840 to 1852, considerable similarity in geographical
patterns is indicated. In general, enough evidence and presumption seems
to exist for its qualified reliability to warrant its use in the analysis of
broad regional patterns.

Having settled on a data source for production, area planted, and
yield for the regional analysis, the question remains how this production
data can be used to develop an indicator for total agricultural production.

The I.S.E.A. data establish that wheat, oats, rye and perhaps barley account for nearly all cereal production. Cereals, possibly along with potatoes and wine, account for most of disposable vegetable production, with straw (from cereals) being one of the two components of total vegetable production produced in larger quantities. Vegetable production, in turn, accounts for roughly three-fourths of total agricultural production. It follows that an index composed of wheat, oats, rye, barley and potatoes would represent a sizeable proportion of total agricultural production.

While these 5 crops represent the major proportion of agricultural production nationally, it is possible that the exclusion of other crops may bias some regions more than others. Wine, and especially corn are found primarily in the southern part of France, leading to a relative understatement of production in those areas. Vegetables and cash crops are found primarily in the North. On balance the exclusion of wine and corn is probably more important. Although exclusion of these crops may bias differentials in regional levels, the effect of the bias on trends may not be so great. Figures 5 and 6 show the growth in corn and wine to closely parallel cereal growth at least through 1870. It is possible, however, for the exclusion of crops to bias trends as well as levels. If there is a growing trend towards crop diversification -- a movement out of crops included and into crops excluded, the result will be a downward bias on the growth of both area cultivated and production.

One major component of total production excluded that might cause concern is animal production, especially meat and milk, and perhaps butter and cheese. As the only data on animals are head counts for widely scattered dates, any estimate of animal production must be indirect. Further, use of gross animal production introduces problems of double counting as various proportions of vegetable crops are not final production, but rather feed for animals.

The procedure used in this study is to retain animal feed (and seed) in the cereal and potato production under the hypothesis that the feed is a reliable estimator of the value of animal production. This hypothesis is dependent on several assumptions: (1) the proportion of feed in the production of cereals and potatoes is constant for each crop over time; (2) the composition of both vegetable and animal production remains fairly constant over the period; and (3) the transformation of feed into animal products remains stable.

The assumption of a constant % feed is born out for wheat by two independent studies for 1862 and for 1938 each of which found 3% of wheat used for feed. Toutain feels that proportion holds back at least to 1845.[6] His figures imply 40% of potatoes used for feed in 1862; he calculates 41% feed for potatoes for 1935-57.[7] In general, his study estimates 17% of all vegetable crops are used for animal feed for the

---

[6]Toutain, op. cit., pp. 47-50.

[7]Ibid.

period 1845-1874, and assumes it holds back to 1815-1845 as well.[8]

It has already been shown that the structure of output remains fairly stable over the period.

Toutain calculates the ratio of production in kilos of cereals to the kilos of hoofed animals (excluding pigs) for 1862 at .5419 and for 1938 at .6262. Assuming that pigs are the only animals eating potatoes, he similarly calculates the ratio of potato production to kilos of pigs at 4823 in both 1845-54 and 1855-64 and at 5522 in 1865-72. He concludes that the transformation of feed into animal production was quite uniform well into the twentieth century.[9] Goreux finds that "in 1882, the value of vegetable output was highly correlated with the weight of livestock per department." He gives the result of the regression: "P/N = 19.4 + .09 Lv/N   R= .75."[10]

What evidence is available seems to indicate that the feed component of vegetable production, and even of cereals and potatoes alone, provides

---

[8]Ibid., p. 55.

[9]Ibid., pp. 47-50.

[10]Louis Goreux, Agricultural Productivity and Economic Development in France, 1852-1950, (Michigan: Ann Arbor Microfilms), p. 41.

a good indicator of animal production.[11]

Aside from the question of an indicator for animal production, the other possible source of serious difficulty is trade, either international or interdepartmental. Apparently neither type of trade is of major significance in the period in question. Net imports of vegetable production in proportion to total vegetable production varies from -8.3% to 19.7% for the period in question, and the assumption can be made that much of the trade primarily effects the cities.[12] Delefortrie and Morice in their study of departmental incomes for 1864 and 1954 make the assumption that transportation is so poorly developed by 1862 that the assumption of no interdepartmental trade can justifiably be made.[13]

Having established a case for the use of the data base, and the use of wheat, oats, rye, barley and potatoes as an indicator of total agricultural production, the issue of how those crops should be aggregated still remains. Two sets of weights are considered here: prices and calories. The decision is made to use calorie weights, primarily because

---

[11]Jean Pautard, Les Disparites Regionales dans la Croissance de L'Agriculture Frandarse (Paris: Gauthier-Villars, 1965), p. 27. He finds that "as poor an indicator of total agricultural production as it may be, it is acceptable to use vegetable production with feed included as an estimator of the value of animal production," citing M. Brousse and Pellier's use in Production agricole et consommation alimentaire de la France 1892-1939, 1944.

[12]Toutain, op. cit., p. 233.

[13]N. Delefortrie and Morice, Les revenues departementaux en 1864 et en 1953 (Paris: 1959), A. Colin, p. 16.

of anticipated analysis of the effect of economic change on demographic change, where the production for own-consumption determines well-being by caloric intake more than cash intake.

The use of calories as weights in aggregating agricultural production has good precedence in the literature:[14] Colin Clark, for example, uses it in his work on subsistence agriculture. Difficulties with price weights are that the regional variations are greater than for calories, and that these regional differences are hard to document. On the national level, it turns out that prices and calories give almost identical weights.

The procedure for determining calorie weight uses the Food and Agricultural Organization's food balance sheet[15] for France for 1960/1 to 1962/3. For each crop, the rate of conversion of kilograms per year into calories per day is calculated. Table I presents these conversion rates for each crop, along with their implicit relative weights.

---

[14]C. Clark and M. Maswell, The Economics of Subsistence Agriculture (London: 1964), Pautard, op. cit., p. 31; F.A.O. Production Yearbook, annual; M. Cépède, "La mesure de la productivite en agriculture," Revue de Ministere de l'Agriculture, May 1959.

[15]F.A.O., Production Yearbook 1964 (Rome: 1964).

TABLE I

Conversion Rates into Calories by Crop

CROP	CONVERSION RATE	WEIGHT
wheat	9.56	1
oats	10.00	1
rye	10.00	1
barley	10.00	1
potatoes	1.92	.2

These relative weights may be crudely tested against price weights by comparing the price per quintal of all cereals (19.45) with the price per quintal of potatoes (3.92) in 1803-12.[16] (The low relative weight for potatoes comes from its high waste water content.)

As the production data employed is in volume units (hectoliters), it is important to know whether the weight of the cereals per unit volume remains constant over the period. Marc Bloch asserts that the average weight of a hectoliter of wheat did not vary significantly from 1815 to 1873.[17]

The procedure adopted for calculating an indicator for total regional agricultural output is to sum the production of wheat, oats, rye, barley and one-fifth potatoes, retaining both feed and seed in the production figures. Summing the hectares planted in each crop gives an indicator of the total land input. Dividing the land total into the production total

[16]Toutain, op. cit., p. 188.

[17]M. Bloch, Statistique de la France, II (Paris: 1876), p. 45.

gives the indicator for average yields.

Figure 7 presents graphs for the total agricultural production of France

for 1815-24 to 1865-74 using both the I.S.E.A. calculation of final real

agricultural product and the indicator of total agricultural production cal-

culated by summing production of wheat, oats, rye, barley and one-fifth

potatoes. The ratio of the indicator of production to the I.S.E.A. final

real production plotted in Figure 7 shows that the indicator grows slightly

more rapidly to 1840, and slightly less rapidly after 1840. The overall

trend for the period 1820 to 1870 is effectively identical, however,

suggesting that the indicator is useful for long trends, but less reliable

for fluctuations. The similarity of the trends in the indicator, which is

based solely on departmental data, and the I.S.E.A. figures, which are

based on census figures where they are available, lends support to re-

liability of the departmental data.

The estimation of the total labor input involves more tenuous assum-

tions. Official statistics on the active agricultural labor force for the

departments do not start before 1851, when they appear infrequently.

Even then, these figures suffer from the normal problems of the unreli-

ability of the estimate of female labor force participation.

Utilizing the knowledge that in the first half of the nineteenth century

most of France is highly agricultural, varying from 61.3% in 1815-24 to

51.3% in 1865-74,[18] and being more concerned with available labor

---

[18]Toutain, op. cit., pp. 200-201.

Figure 7

France: Agricultural Production, I.S.E.A. Data
and Calorie Deflated Estimates

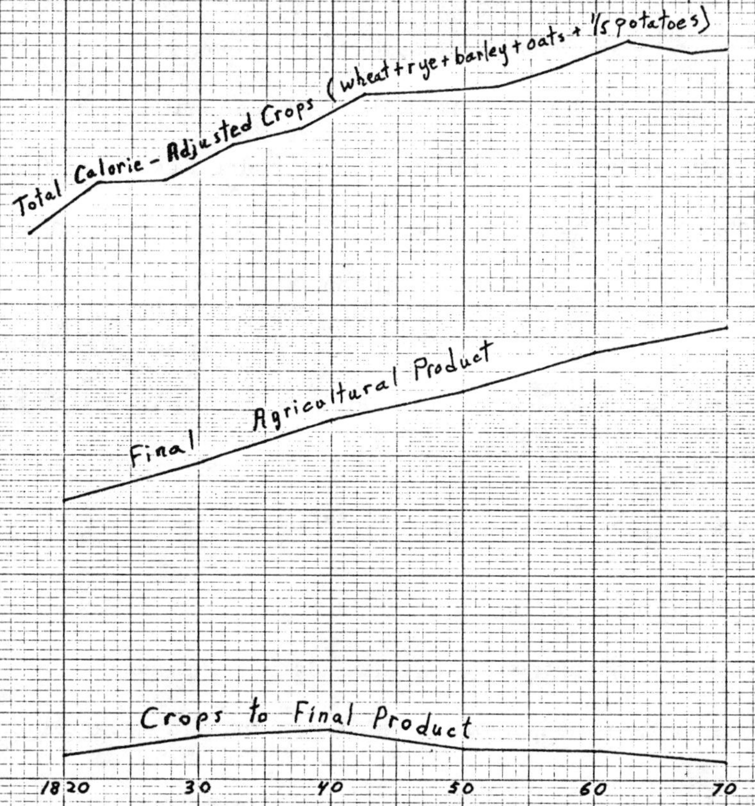

supply than questions of unemployment, the indicator adopted is an estimator for rural population.

The estimator for rural population is calculated for each department by subtracting from the total population the population of cities which by 1876 had reached a size of 20,000 or larger. While this estimator clearly leaves much to be desired, it provides the only means of gaining any insight into gross trends in available regional labor inputs.

The procedure used by Toutain to obtain his national estimates is to assume that the male agricultural labor force remains a constant 20% of the rural population. He uses estimates of Boislandry and Gaudin for rural population in 1815 and the official rural population estimates for 1851 and interpolates for the intervening years.[19] Figure 8 compares the potential labor force estimate used here with Toutain's estimate. The trends are quite similar up to 1860 or 1870 when Toutain's estimate begins to decline less rapidly, providing some support for the estimate used here.

C. Regional Differences from the National Pattern

It is useful to begin the regional analysis by reviewing the national patterns, using the same methods of calculation that are employed for the regions. Figure 9 presents these graphs.

National production grows rapidly from 1820 to 1860, or 1870, stagnating thereafter; growth is faster in the period up to 1840, than from

---

[19]Ibid.

Figure 8

France: Agricultural Production and Labor Force

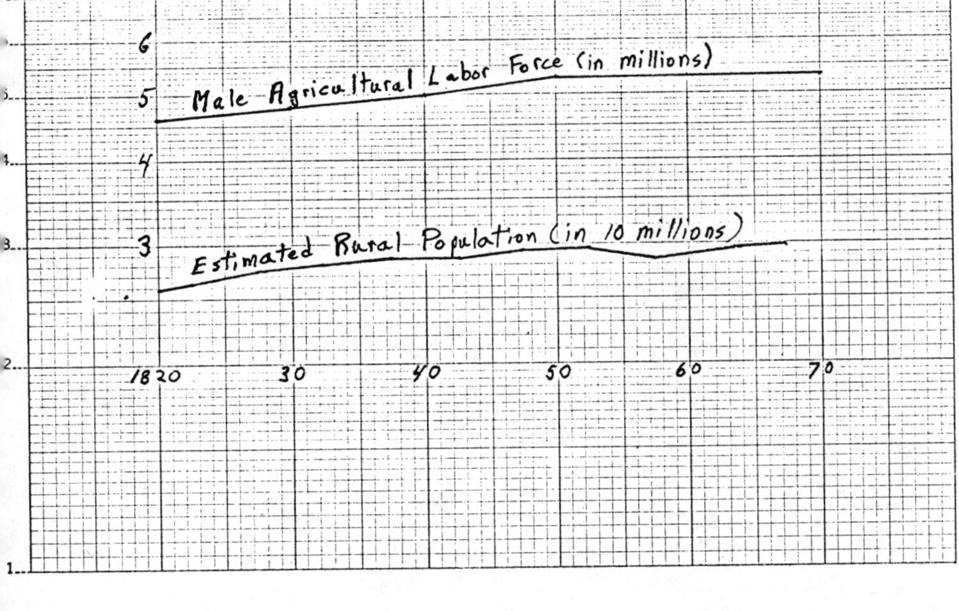
6
5
4
3
2
1
Male Agricultural Labor Force (in millions)
Estimated Rural Population (in 10 millions)
1820
30
40
50
60
70

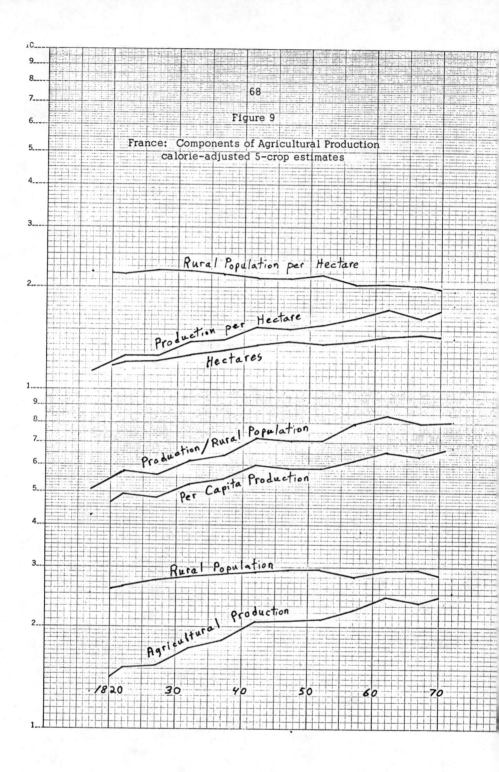

68

Figure 9

France: Components of Agricultural Production
calorie-adjusted 5-crop estimates

1840 on. The faster growth to 1840 may reflect bias in the measure of output employed, as this measure shows faster growth during this period than the comprehensive I.S.E.A. figures. Population growth is slow through the century, with slightly faster growth before the 1840's than after. Consequently, per capita production growth is rapid to 1840, and slow to 1860, where it ends for the century.

Land inputs grow slowly to 1845, and imperceptibly thereafter. Labor inputs (rural population) grow slowly to 1845, remain constant to 1865, then decline.

Productivity of both land and labor grow rapidly to 1870, stagnating thereafter, with labor productivity growing slightly faster.

The ratio of labor to land inputs declines slowly throughout the period.

I.S.E.A. figures for the same period show the man/land ratio rising. This difference is due both to the more rapid growth in the labor input and the less rapid growth in the land input in the I.S.E.A. estimates. The faster growth of land under the five crops than under all crops suggests that some of the growth in land under the five crops may represent substitution for other crops. In that case, the decline in the man/land ratio may be overstated. On the other hand, there is some reason to believe that the growth in the I.S.E.A. estimate of the labor input may be overstated. It is unlikely that agricultural labor force would grow significantly faster than rural population. Yet, the I.S.E.A. estimates for agricultural labor force show it growing as fast as total population. The rural population trend is probably a pretty good estimator of the trend in the potential supply of labor in agriculture, if not the actual labor force. If the I.S.E.A. figures overstate the growth in agricultural labor force, then the growth in the man/land ratio using their figures is overstated. While the two estimates of the man/land ratio are conflicting, when the biases of each are examined, the conclusion seems to be that the man/land ratio is more constant than either estimate suggests.

In general, a similar national picture emerges overall with these estimates as with the I.S.E.A. figures. The differences in timing of the most rapid growth in production may represent upward bias in these estimates before 1840. And the differences in the estimates of the man/land ratio are largely differences in the drift of a basically constant ratio.

Now, however, the national picture can be extended because figures are available on land input by crop. Figure 10 presents the area under cultivation in hectares for each crop. The total land input conceals important differences in land input by crop: cultivation of potatoes, wheat and oats expands; rye and barley cultivation contracts. Comparing Figure 10 with the crop production trends for cereals in Figure 5 indicates that the production differentials by crop are largely determined by differentials in the land input. This suggests that productivity trends by crop must be much more alike than the trends in land inputs.

Figure 11 gives the trends in yields (land productivity or production/

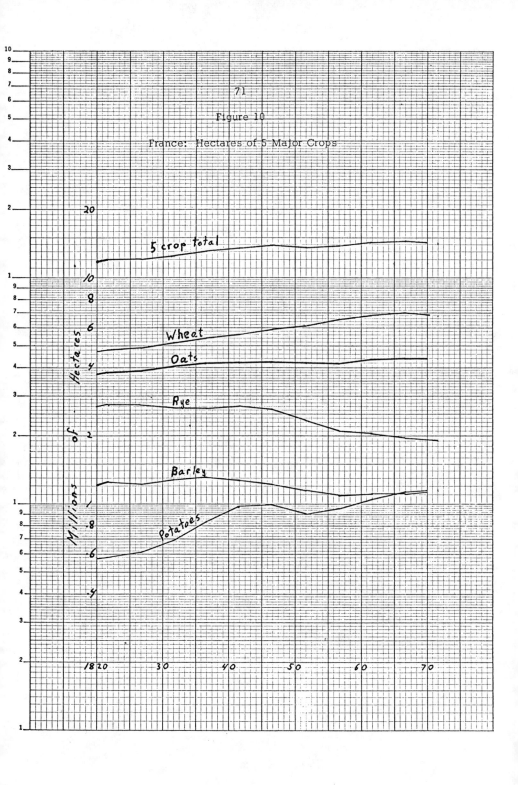

71

Figure 10

France: Hectares of 5 Major Crops

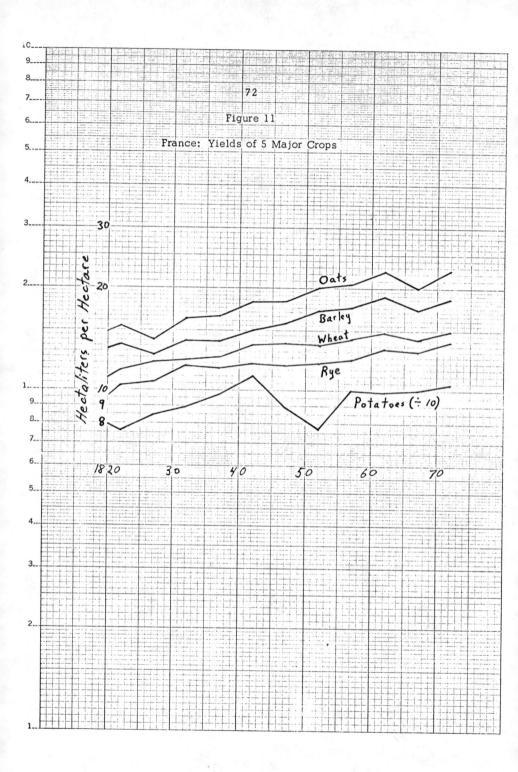

72

Figure 11

France: Yields of 5 Major Crops

hectare) by crop. The four cereal crops display a considerable similarity in trends, while potato yields differ greatly. The yields for potatoes fluctuate over a wide range (due in part to the potato bug invasion in 1846) but seem to exhibit no clear trend. It might be argued, however, that the early growth in yields associated with the initial widespread introduction of the potato constitutes a trend. The interesting feature of Figure 11 is the uniformity of growth in the yields of cereal crops: yields for all cereals grow steadily and rapidly to 1860, then (except for rye, and for wheat after the late 1870's) they maintain that level. One explanation for the continued growth in rye yields might be that the contraction of land under rye cultivation is from marginal lands with lower than average pro-ductivity, allowing average rye yields to climb to the average for wheat.

The similarity in the trends of growth in yields hides an important difference, however. In the period up to 1860, growth in yields of oats and barley is greater than for wheat and rye. Rates of growth are almost identical for oats and barley, as are the fluctuations around the trend. Similarly, growth rates are very close for wheat and rye, although some difference appears in fluctuations. And in the period after 1860, yields of rye and to some extent wheat, continue to grow while barley and oats yields remain constant.

The regional variations from the national pattern for growth in pro-duction by crop are summarized in Table II. The regional classification employed here is the scheme developed in Chapter I. This scheme was developed to display differential demographic behavior. Regions are classified by the proportion of their population living from agriculture (numeric classification) and the height of the birth rate at the turn of the century (the alphabetic classification). Thus regions 3 have a lower % agriculture than regions 4, and regions 4 are lower yet than regions 5. Regions A have the low initial birth rates; regions B have high initial birth rates. A rough geographical pattern emerges from this classification scheme as well: high % agriculture is found in the South, medium % agriculture is found in the center, and low % agriculture in the North (see Figure 3, Chapter I). Regions 1 and 2 are excluded from the analysis in this chapter because they include only major urban centers -- Paris, and Marseille and Lyon, respectively, where agricultural production is negligible. Figures in the table represent percentage change from 1815-9 to 1860-4, calculated as follows: $(1860-4 - 1815-9) \div \boxed{(1860-4 + 1815-9) \div \underline{2}}$, so the denominator is the arithmetic mean of initial and terminal observations.

Reading the bottom (All Crops) row of Table II shows that all regions share fairly uniformly in the growth in total agricultural production in France. While much greater regional diversity from the national pattern is observed for individual crops (reading across the other rows), the crops exhibiting the most important growth -- wheat, potatoes, and oats, have much more regional uniformity.

The column for France indicates as mentioned that wheat, potatoes,

TABLE II

Regional Production Growth by Crop

(Percentage Change 1815-9 to 1860-4)

Crop	3A	3B	4A	4B	5A	5B	France
Wheat	63.11	60.82	90.98	86.17	60.77	61.44	75.15
Rye	17.34	25.98	-11.24	22.10	41.48	42.86	22.00
Potatoes	70.71	83.16	71.22	83.89	88.70	56.92	74.90
Oats	59.16	60.05	78.93	65.29	25.42	57.12	63.22
Barley	34.47	09.68	52.43	31.44	-01.51	68.97	39.39
All Crops	57.72	60.81	74.69	66.20	51.71	55.42	63.46

and oats grow much more rapidly than rye and barley. This pattern of relative crop growth holds for regions 3 and 4, but breaks down for regions 5.

Table III summarizes the regional variations in the components in total output. Calculations are the same as in Table II.

The last column of Table III shows that growth in productivity accounts for much more of the national growth in output than do the growth in inputs: productivity growth is two or three times as great as input growth. Land and labor grow at roughly similar rates, with the slightly faster growth in the land input causing the man/land ratio to move downward a little.

While the relative importance of input growth and productivity growth varies from region to region, for all regions the growth in productivity is

TABLE III

Growth in Components of Regional Total Production

(Percentage Change from 1815-9 to 1860-4)

Component	3A	3B	4A	4B	5A	5B	France
Output	57.72	60.81	74.69	66.20	51.71	55.43	63.46
Land	13.66	25.60	27.04	28.50	09.50	23.51	23.07
Labor	13.61	21.72	12.57	17.69	12.98	12.00	15.37
Land Pro- ductivity	44.94	36.60	50.17	38.62	42.71	44.06	41.96
Labor Pro- ductivity	44.99	40.43	63.61	49.97	39.38	44.16	49.30
Land/Labor	.00	-03.94	-14.60	-10.95	03.50	-11.60	-07.77

substantially more important than growth in inputs. The change in the
land-labor ratio varies noticeably from region to region, but in no region
is the change very large.

General uniformity in the regional growth of both inputs and produc-
tivities underlies the observed uniformity in regional output growth.

Table IV shows the relative importance for each region of land input
and land productivity in the growth of the crops displaying the most rapid
growth in production. Labor inputs are not included because there is no
way to apportion the labor force among the various crops.

For the nation wheat, potatoes, and oats each display a different
pattern of composition of output growth. Balanced growth in land input

TABLE IV

Growth in Components of Regional Production for Selected Crops

(Percentage Change from 1815-9 to 1860-4)

WHEAT	3A	3B	4A	4B	5A	5B	France
Output	63.11	60.82	90.98	86.17	60.77	61.44	75.15
Hectares	30.34	26.12	47.78	52.95	14.72	32.72	39.25
Yield	34.16	36.12	48.34	37.57	46.99	29.84	38.73
POTATOES	3A	3B	4A	4B	5A	5B	France
Output	70.71	83.16	71.22	83.89	88.70	56.92	74.90
Hectares	71.45	67.10	65.80	57.98	36.49	71.08	61.58
Yield	-01.25	18.48	05.66	29.21	56.79	-16.05	14.76
OATS	3A	3B	4A	4B	5A	5B	France
Output	59.16	60.05	78.93	65.29	25.42	57.12	63.22
Hectares	07.49	22.77	24.04	29.92	00.29	21.62	18.63
Yield	52.27	38.60	57.63	37.16	25.11	36.63	45.91

and productivity underlies the growth in wheat; growth in land input accounts for almost all of the growth in potatoes; and output growth in oats results primarily from the growth in land productivity. These patterns of the relative importance of the sources of growth in production hold consistently for all three crops for every region except 5A, where productivity growth dominates in every crop, thus departing from the patterns for wheat and potatoes, and 4B which has a significantly higher proportion of the growth in wheat due to growth in hectares.

The next section explores more carefully the conclusions drawn from the regional summary tables. Figures 12 to 17 present the regional graphs for each of the components of total agricultural production. The conclusion that production growth is similar for all regions from 1815-1870 is only partly born out in Figure 12. Regions 4 experience usually rapid growth before 1840, while region 5B grows less rapidly than the rest of France through 1860-70, and then begins to catch up late in the century.

Figure 13 indicates that while roughly the same growth pattern in land inputs holds across the regions, faster growth in hectares planted accounts for the rapid early growth in regions 4.

While similar patterns do hold in Figure 14 for rural population (labor input), in the last half of the period of rapid growth regions 5 (the most agricultural) reach a peak earlier and decline faster.

Figure 15 reveals generally similar yield patterns except for a lagged growth in region 5B, with no growth to 1850 followed by important growth late in the century.

In Figure 16 region 5B also exhibits catchup growth in labor productivity. The regional uniformity observed in the other components is somewhat less evident here, although all regions experience important growth during the period.

Two basic patterns emerge from the regional labor/land ratios in Figure 17: regions 3A, 3B and 5A remain fairly constant; regions 4A, 4B and 5B exhibit noticeable declines.

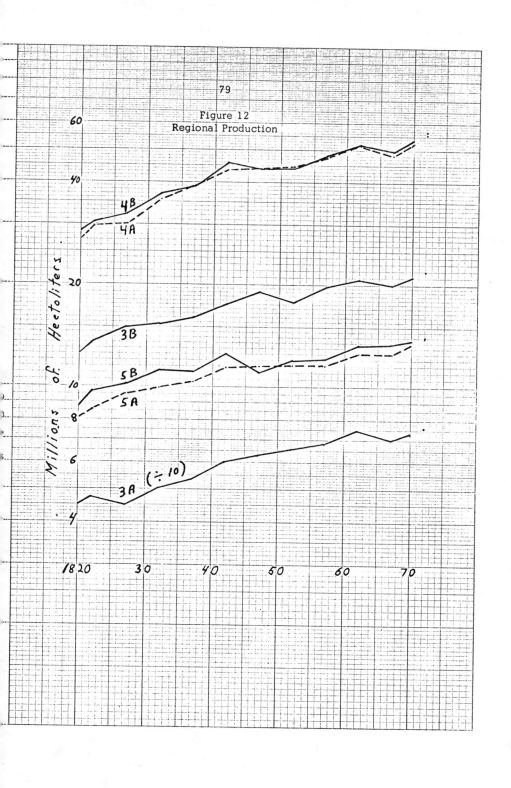

79

Figure 12
Regional Production

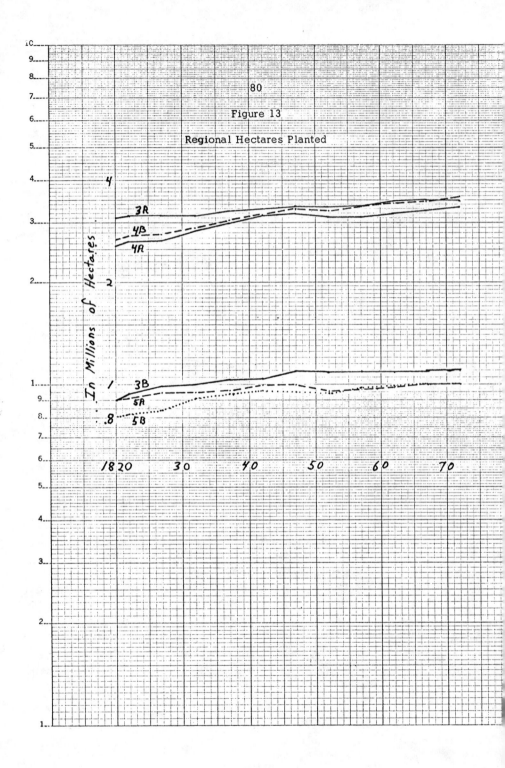

80

Figure 13

Regional Hectares Planted

Figure 14
Regional Rural Population (in millions)

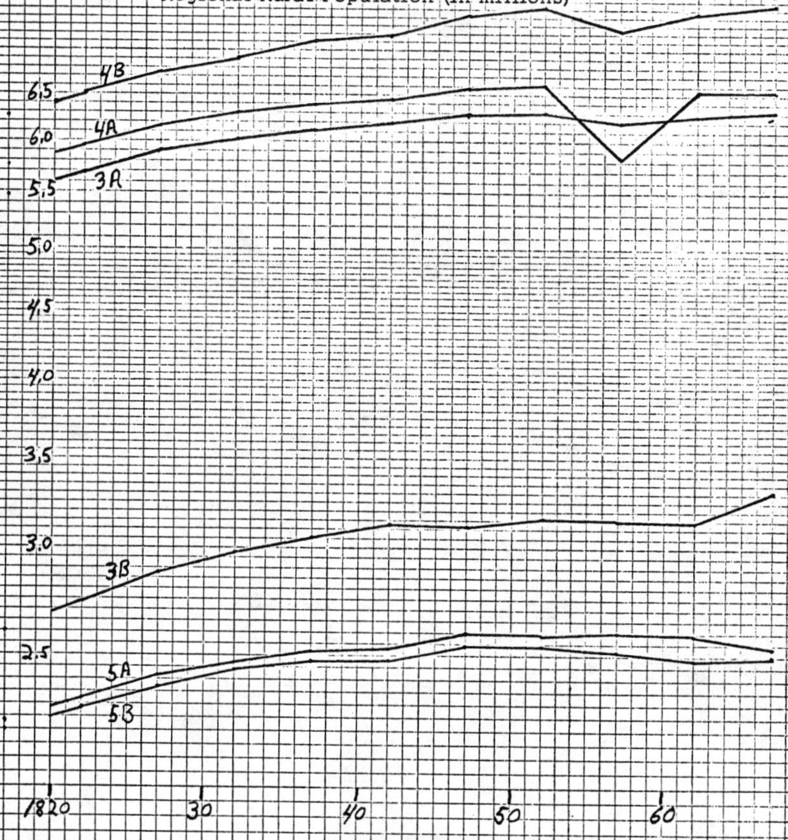

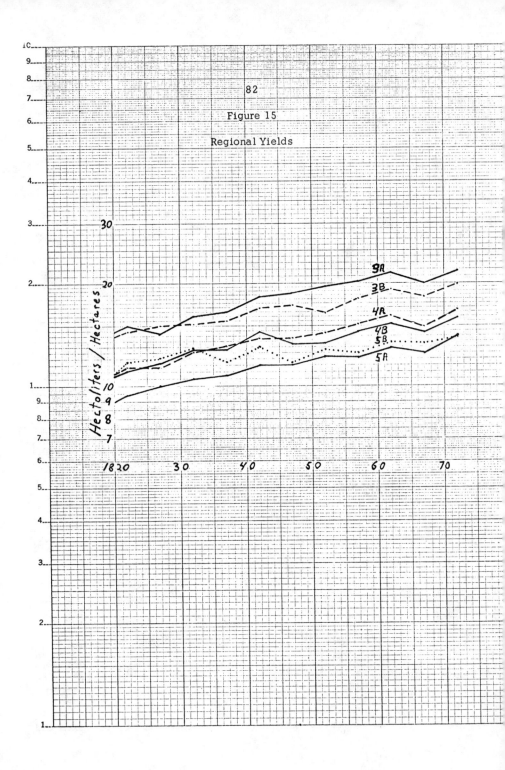

82

Figure 15

Regional Yields

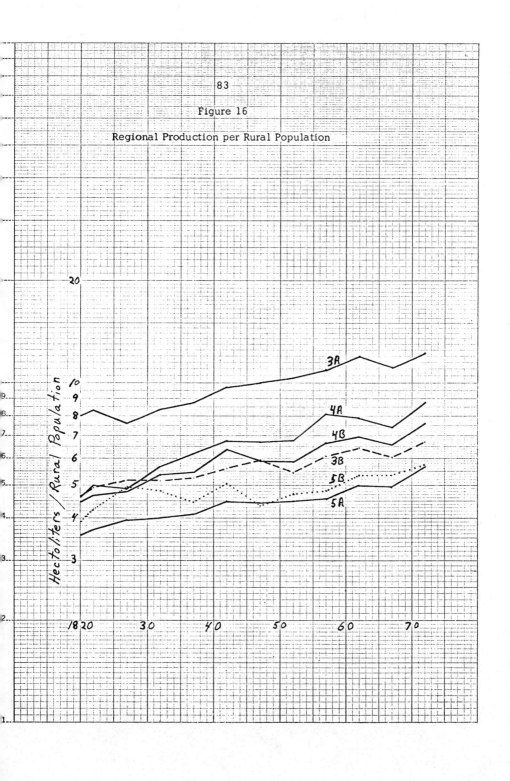

83

Figure 16

Regional Production per Rural Population

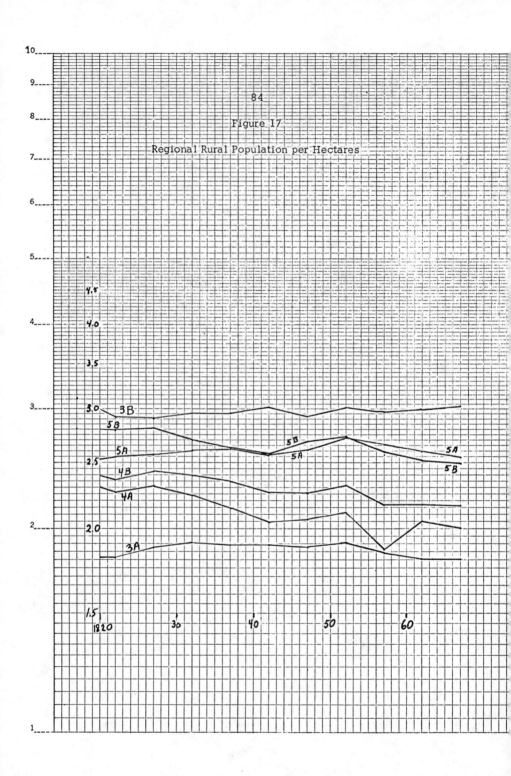

84

Figure 17

Regional Rural Population per Hectares

PART II. RE-EXAMINATION OF THE TIMING OF THE AGRICULTURAL
REVOLUTION

The picture of agricultural development in nineteenth century France

presented in this chapter contrasts sharply with the traditional discussion

of the timing and the nature of the agricultural revolution -- the changes

in the productive process causing sustained rapid growth in both total and

per capita agricultural production.

The following selection from Clapham's popular treatise, Economic

Development of France and Germany 1815-1914 of 1921 to 1936, captures

well the spirit of this view:

> A French scholar writing, just after the middle of the
> nineteenth century, about the medieval agriculture of a
> progressive French province, called his readers' atten-
> tion to "the stationary state in which our agriculture has
> remained during nearly eight centuries. Almost all the
> methods which we shall describe," he said, "are
> practiced by our cultivators today; so that a thirteenth
> century peasant would visit many of our farms without
> much astonishment."[20]

> When Leopold Delisle wrote, in 1852, of how little
> French agriculture had changed since the thirteenth
> century, France had several railways but no railway
> system. In the next ten years the railways grew into a
> system and the telegraph came. French agriculture did
> not forthwith cease to be in many ways medieval...But
> forces were set free vastly more powerful than had ever
> played upon it, forces capable of doing in decades what
> under previous conditions might have taken centuries.[21]

---

[20]J. H. Clapham, Economic Development of France and Germany 1815-
1914, 4th edition, reprinted 1966 (England: Cambridge U.), p. 6.

[21]Ibid., p. 158.

M. Augé-Laribé, writing in 1912, selects 1860 as the beginning of modern French agriculture, citing mechanization, foreign competition, and rising costs of production as underlying causes of this agricultural modernization.[22] And in La Révolution Agricole of 1955 Augé-Laribé draws a broad periodization of French agriculture: 1600-1815, traditional agriculture; 1815-1871, a period of preparation and transition; and 1871 on, modern agriculture. This last period is distinguished by continual improvement in the techniques of production and distribution.[23]

Writing of this situation in France in 1846, Clough asserts:[24] "In the North and in the valley of the Garonne, the agricultural revolution was well under way. In these districts, the three-field system...was disappearing." But he concludes "Only after the middle of the /nineteenth/ century did fundamental changes become general."

Henri Sée, one of the greatest French economic historians, writes (my translation):

> From 1840, progress was more marked than before, and manifested itself in all regions of France. By the late 1850's, a major project was completed to drain the swamps in Seine-Inferieure; in the 1850's, fallow land completely disappeared from Haute-Normandy. In Bas-Maine, one of the most backward areas of France, a real agricultural revolution was experienced after 1840: liming, decline in fallow land, growth in hectares planted in wheat and a

---

[22]M. Augé-Laribé, L'évolution de la france agricole, 1912.

[23]M. Augé-Laribé, La révolution agricole, 1955.

[24]S. Clough, France 1789-1939, 1939.

decline in rye and buckwheat, growth in artificial
meadows, and better quality animals. Similar developments occurred in Ille-et-Vilaine. [25]

While the emphasis varies with the author, the general pattern is
clear. Around midcentury -- from the 1840's to 1860 -- French agriculture underwent or at least began modernization. For many this means the
completion of the interrelated set of reforms urged by the agronomes since
the 1750's -- the elimination of fallow and the institution of the scientific
crop rotation of mixed farming, allowing the production of legumes and
forage crops on artifical and natural meadows. These in turn provide
winter stall feeding for farm animals, which provide manure (along with
lime and other artifical fertilizers) to raise yields, motive power to pull
heavy farm implements to raise the area under cultivation, and meat to
improve the diet. For many, it means the exposure of French agriculture
to the rigors of foreign competition. For most all, it means the impact of
the industrial revolution, whether through better transportation by railroads
or faster communication through the telegraph, or most common, the
mechanization of agriculture.

This traditional view does not entirely exclude, however, the existence of change in French agriculture from the Revolution to 1850. Indeed,
all the economic historians that are referred to in this study who deal with
that period, recognize that changes are taking place. Some even say that

---

[25]H. Sée, La Vie Économique de la France sous la Monarchie
Censitaire 1815-1848, 1927.

they are important developments. However, all find these changes to be relatively less significant than those that occur after midcentury. Developments which are generally recognized to have taken place before 1850 are as follows: the expansion of the arable; the introduction of the potato; the beginning of the elimination of fallow and the use of artifical meadows; growth in the number of livestock; some minor improvements in farm implements; some improvement in sheep breeding; and the extension of a few industrial crops. But with the exception of the introduction of the potato, all of these developments are assumed to have taken place almost exclusively in the North around Paris, and in the far North near Flanders.

While these authors all wrote before the publication of Toutain's study for the I.S.E.A. in 1961, they all had available the data which not only form the primary source for at least the period 1815 to 1840, but also provide the basis for this study.

Although Toutain provides very little interpretation of the evidence in his study, he does split the nineteenth century into three phases of growth in real agricultural production: 1815-24 to 1834-44, increasing growth; 1835-44 to 1875-84, slow growth; and 1885-1894 to World War I, recovery.[26] He represents 1815 as the first major long-term turning point, with the next one in 1914. He sees these turning points as representing basic structural shifts.[27]

---

[26]Toutain, op. cit., p. 122.

[27]Ibid., p. 138.

The impact on the literature of this extensive compilation of empirical evidence is curious.

Rondo Cameron, writing in 1965 on French economic development, simply ignores the available empirical evidence: "Agriculture, it is true, made relatively little progress in either technology or output, at least before 1840."[28]

And in 1968, Barral asserts that after 1851, urban demand and the railroads created outlets for growth in cereals and animal production, and the price of food went up, resulting in the growth in agriculture.[29]

Kindleberger, on the other hand, sees one "agricultural revolution" from the mid-eighteenth to the mid-nineteenth century based on the suggested reforms of the agronomes and another "agricultural revolution" after the mid-nineteenth century based on mechanization, artificial fertilizers, and railroads -- what I have called the "traditional view." And within that latter revolution he sees a "virtual revolution in food consumption" with the relative growth in meat products. To substantiate this eclectic view, he quotes the 1952 I.S.E.A. study[30] which he says suggests a growth in agricultural production of 1.8%/year for 1850 to

---

[28]Rondo Cameron, France and the Economic Development of Europe 1800-1914, 2nd edition (Chicago: Rand McNally, 1965), p. 52.

[29]Pierre Barral, Les Agrariens Francais de Méline à Pisani, (Paris: 1968), p. 67.

[30]Francois Pérroux, "Prise de veues sur la croissance de l'économie francaise, 1780-1950," Income and Wealth, V., 1955, pp. 41-78.

1880, following a growth of only 1%/year for the period 1788 to 1850. (He ignores the fact that the virtual stagnation in agriculture from 1788 to 1815 conceals the very rapid growth from 1815 to 1850.) He then uses this discussion of important growth and an agricultural revolution before 1850 to prove that French agriculture of that period was "not...entirely static." He then states that French agriculture was generally backward, concluding that "French economic growth as a whole has been held back by the slowness of advance in agriculture."[31]

Writing in 1965 on the regional differentials in the growth of French agriculture, Jean Pautard summarizes the national trends which he gleans from both I.S.E.A. studies and various other empirical sources. He sees slow growth from 1790 to 1840, with the growth from 1790-1815 twice as rapid as from 1815-1840, and rapid growth from 1840 to 1890, with no growth to 1848 and the fastest growth from 1852 to 1862.[32] I cannot explain how he uses either I.S.E.A. study to support this national pattern of growth. But he does recognize Toutain as a major source for this period. He then goes on to assert that the regional data before the enquetes are worthless, ignoring the fact that the I.S.E.A. studies which he accepts arrive at their national trends by aggregating the same regional data he declares worthless. By ignoring the regional data before 1840, he

[31]Charles Kindleberger, Economic Growth in France and Britain: 1851-1950 (New York: Simon & Schuster, 1965), pp. 211-217.

[32]Pautard, op. cit., p. 39.

feels he is able to assert that "regional variation was relatively weak" (my translation) around 1800, because the regions were equalized in their mediocrity.[33]

It is clear that the important contributions to the development of statistical evidence on the trends in French agriculture have had little impact on the traditional view of the agricultural revolution in France.

This misunderstanding of the development of French agriculture has had important bearing on the overall interpretation of French economic history since the Revolution. As has been seen in the discussion of Kindleberger, the acceptance of no important growth in agriculture before 1850 leads to the conclusion that growth in total national production was achieved only through the late, uneven growth in the relatively small industrial sector, with agriculture acting as a large hinderance to economic progress.

If the traditional view of the agricultural revolution persists in the face of empirical evidence, and the possibility of ignorance of that evidence is removed by references to it, the question must arise why the view does not change.

One possible source of explanation must lie in price movements. Figure 18 shows the movement in the general price index and its effect on the trend in total agricultural production, as calculated by Toutain.[34] The

---

[33]Ibid., pp. 67-8.

[34]Toutain, op. cit., pp. 64, 128-9, 269.

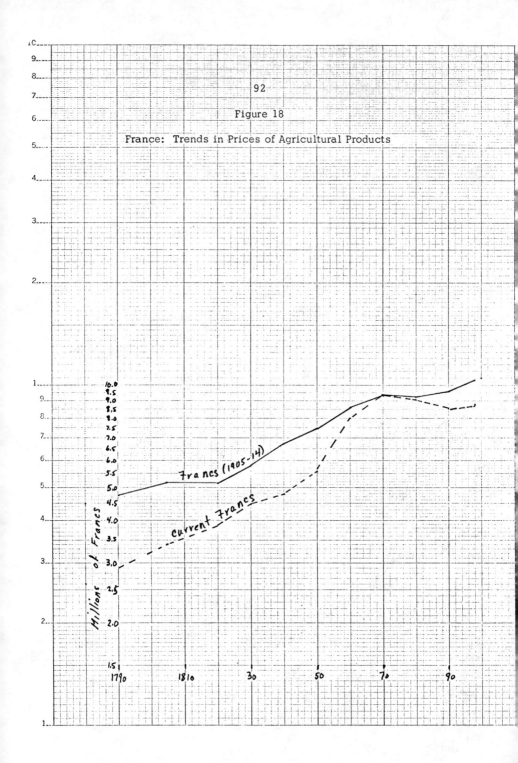

Figure 18

France: Trends in Prices of Agricultural Products

price level takes a sharp upward turn from 1850 to 1870. As a result total product in current francs grows faster from 1840 or 1850 to 1870 than any other period before the twentieth century. If production is not deflated, the trend in production is more nearly what is expected from the literature, although growth is substantial all the way from 1750 to 1840-50. This explanation, however, is hardly convincing, because all the emphasis in Toutain's study is on the deflated series, and the conclusions on major turning points use deflated data and point to 1815 and 1914 as the times of greatest structural change.

Another explanation might be that the traditional view is based on the timing of the decline in fallow and the growth in artificial meadows. These developments are central to the change to the scientific crop rotation of mixed farming which could be responsible for important growth in both area under cultivation and yields. And it is true that dramatic declines in fallow and great additions to artificial meadows came after mid-century. However, fallow declined 2.4 million hectares, or 30% from 1781-1790 to 1845-54, and the interruption of the Revolution and the Napoleonic wars lends credence to the hypothesis that almost all declines came after 1815. And while artificial meadows were starting from a low base, they increased 1.5 million hectares, or over 100% from 1815-24 to 1845-54. Compare these figures to the 30 year period after midcentury: 1845-54 to 1875-84. Fallow declines by 36%, a slightly greater percentage drop, but by only 2.1 million hectares, a smaller absolute decline. Artificial meadows increase by 1.6 million hectares, about the same absolute increase, but only by 57%.[35] These figures demonstrate that, at best, the period after midcentury continues the change in crop rotation which has been in progress at least since 1815.

A more plausible explanation lies in the biases of those representing the traditional view. Everyone knows, so the thinking seems to run, that modernization in agriculture comes from railroads (creating wider markets and providing cheaper transportation), mechanization in agriculture (the combines in America at the time), use of artificial fertilizers, scientific breeding of animals; and every enlightened economist knows that high protective tariffs hamper growth by lowering incentives for efficiency and innovation. Railroads, mechanization, and use of artificial fertilizers all came into French agriculture around midcentury. Further, France had the most protective tariff on agriculture of any country in the world from 1815 to 1860. Every presumption leads to the conclusion that the important changes in French agriculture must have taken place in the last half of the nineteenth century. Naturally, this unkind generalization does not do full justice to everyone. Clapham, for example, makes a strong case that the reaper and other large mechanical implements could not have had an important impact on French agriculture until nearly 1900; yet he places great emphasis on the role of the railroad. Nonetheless, the force of preconceived ideas on the findings of research is well-known, and no other

---

[35]Toutain, op. cit., pp. 214-215.

good explanation readily presents itself.

It is possible to overemphasize the all-pervasive nature of the traditional view, however. One notable exception has quite recently appeared with the publication in late 1969 of Agrarian Change and Economic Development. The article in it by E.J.T. Collins on the demand and supply of labor in European Agriculture from 1800 to 1880[36] uses the Toutain data in a way similar to the national discussion in Part I -- choosing wheat, rye, barley, and oats production with feed and seed included, and adding them with implicitly equal weights. He accepts the view that the important growth in French agriculture occurred before 1850.

Conclusion

The picture that emerges from this chapter is one of important growth in French agriculture in the nineteenth century. The period of most rapid growth seems to come between the end of the Napoleonic Wars in 1815 and the Franco-Prussian War in 1870. While both land and labor inputs experience some growth during this period, that growth is slow and can account for only the smaller part of the growth in output. The bulk of the growth in production is attributable to productivity increases.

Accompanying the growth in output are changes in the relative importance of crops. Rye and barley production decline, while wheat, oats

---

[36]E. Collins, "Labour supply and demand in European agriculture 1800-1880," E. Jones and S. Woolf (eds.), Agrarian Change and Economic Development (London: Methuen, 1969), pp. 61-94.

and potatoes grow in importance. These changes in crop composition primarily reflect changes in the hectares under each crop.

The important growth in yields is shared by all cereal crops observed, but it is unimportant in potatoes. While the growth in yields is quite steady for the entire period for all cereals, significant differences do emerge in the rate of growth: barley and oats grow faster than wheat and rye.

The overall regional picture is one of basic similarity with the national patterns. Some regional differences do exist, however. Regions 4A and 4B (medium % agriculture, and typically from the Center of France) have faster growth than the national average in overall production and in every crop except rye. The slower growth in rye comes from faster declines in rye hectares. Regions 5A and 5B (the most agricultural and generally in the South of France) tend to have the slowest growth in output. This stems from slower growth in productivity. Towards the end of the period of rapid national growth, productivity in these regions increases much faster than the national rate to the levels for the rest of France. Within the national pattern of a mild decline in the man/land ratio, regions 3A and 3B (low % agriculture and mostly Northern) remain fairly constant, while regions 4 and 5 experience more noticeable declines (with region 5A an exception).

The agricultural patterns set out in this chapter contrast sharply with literature on French agricultural development. It is generally accepted that the "agricultural revolution" in France occurred in the last half of the nineteenth century. The consensus is that until roughly midcentury French agriculture had changed little from medieval times.

Although the sources of this supposed revolution in agriculture in the last half of the century vary with the author, commonly cited are industrialization, mechanization in agriculture, artificial fertilizers, and the development of railroads. All these developments do come after midcentury, but they can provide little explanation for the most important agricultural growth which occurred primarily before midcentury. Some argue that the change from old rotation systems to scientific crop rotations might be important in this agricultural revolution. Major declines in fallow and growth of artificial meadows do suggest that a change in rotation systems might indeed underlie much of the growth in agriculture. But these developments do not support the argument that agriculture was stagnant before midcentury, since declines in fallow and growth in artificial meadows are at least as great in the 30 year period before midcentury as in the 30 year period after midcentury.

CHAPTER III

DEMOGRAPHIC RESPONSES TO POPULATION PRESSURE

In Chapter I, we found significant associations between birth and death rates, and between rates of natural increase and net migration. The hypothesis was advanced that the birth rate level was causally related to the death rate: that a lower death rate would lead to a lower birth rate. Similarly, it was suggested that higher rates of natural increase might cause higher rates of net out-migration. These hypotheses are part of a more general hypothesis, examined in this chapter, that population pressure will bring about demographic responses designed to ease that pressure.

The concept of population pressure is ultimately one of the interaction between population and its environment. The argument in its simplest form is that some sort of equilibrium is maintained between population and its environment: if either changes, pressure is created which brings about a new equilibrium. If population grows relative to its environment, the resulting population pressure may bring about a change in either population or environment. This chapter concerns itself only with the demographic responses to that pressure. Chapter IV will deal with economic responses to population pressure.

Review of the Literature

A pioneering statement of the hypothesis that population responds to changes in the balance between population and environment is found in Kingsley Davis's "The Theory of Change and Response in Modern Demographic History."[1] In this article he argues that declining death rates and resulting sustained high rates of natural increase create population pressure to which individual families respond with the full range of demographic alternatives -- delayed marriage, reduced fertility, abortion, and out-migration. Unlike previous arguments which saw such demographic behavior as responses to increasing poverty, he sees the responses for much of Western Europe and Japan resulting from immediate or anticipated erosion of improvements in living standards. These are demographic responses to declines in the growth of real income, or even responses to fears of income decline. Davis sees this pressure operating within the family through larger completed family size, although he is not clear through what mechanism it operates. In agricultural areas he sees this pressure coming largely though problems of land inheritance: "The structure of rural societies was such that they could accomodate permanently growing populations only on one assumption -- territorial expansion."[2] While he sees a "multi-phasic" response in agriculture as well as in

---

[1] K. Davis, "The Theory of Change and Response in Modern Demographic History," Population Index, XXIX, 4 (October, 1963), pp. 345-366.

[2] Ibid., p. 353.

industrialized areas, he finds net migration to be the most important
agricultural response in countries which are industrializing. With expanding urban employment opportunities through industrialization, he
finds little need for extensive fertility control in agricultural areas.

Ryder and Westoff suggest a mechanism by which this pressure gets
translated into demographic response.[3] They argue that families have
some notion of their desired completed family size. Reproductive behavior is controlled to achieve that desired completed family size. High
mortality requires high fertility to achieve the desired family size. With
high infant mortality, fertility may be high relative to desired family size
because a family will conceive additional children to replace ones that
die before adulthood. With declines in infant mortality, an immediate
fall in fertility will occur, to the extent that replacement births are not
longer perceived to be needed. But the probable effect of the mortality
decline will be to raise actual family size relative to desired family size.
When actual family size is perceived to be too large relative to desired
size, the family will limit its fertility. It is this disperity between
desired and actual family size which they see as the mechanism through
which demographic responses come about.

Probably the most controversial assumption Ryder and Westoff make

---

[3]Ryder, Norman B. and Westoff, Charles F., "Relationships among
intended, expected, desired, and ideal family size: United States,
1965." /In series7 Cpr Population Research. Washington, U. S. Center
for Population Research, March, 1969, pp. 7.

is that families do indeed have a desired family size. Ronald Freedman,

in an article[4] based on sample surveys for every major area of the world,

reports that norms for family size are indeed universal, and almost never

at the biological maximum. He finds a collective idea of ideal completed

family size throughout the underdeveloped world.

Davis's article raised the question of which demographic responses

are used under what circumstances. This question is tackled by Fried-

lander in a recent article.[5] Friedlander looks at the growth in labor supply

resulting, with a lag, from the decline in the death rate. The form that

the demographic response takes, he says, depends on the opportunities

for non-agricultural employment. If non-agricultural opportunities are

plentiful, then substantial out-migration will occur and the birth rate will

remain high. If, on the other hand, non-agricultural employment oppor-

tunities are scarce, then the birth rate will fall and out-migration will be

largely unchanged.

Easterlin concludes from observing demographic developments in the

United States that "the American experience raises the possibility that as

population increasingly presses against land resources, fertility declines

---

[4]R. Freedman, "Norms for Family Size in Underdeveloped Areas" in Proceedings of the Royal Society, B., Vol. 159 (London, 1963), pp. 220-245.

[5]D. Friedlander, "Demographic Responses and Population Change" in Demography, Vol. 6, no. 4, November, 1969.

may set in within the rural sector itself."[6] This rural fertility decline

occurred within a country with substantial agricultural opportunities and

where non-agricultural opportunities became great well before the fertility

decline was completed.

This literature suggests a plausible mechanism through which demo-

graphic changes can be expected in response to population pressure on

the environment. It also presents considerable historical demographic

evidence to support the contention that population adjusts to the environ-

ment. However, it is still not clear which responses will occur in which

situations, and how strong different responses will be. And while the

experience of many different countries is presented, there is no systematic

attempt to test, statistically, the hypotheses presented.

The mechanism suggested in this literature by which population can

be expected to adjust to the environment raises a serious question about

the French experience. In other countries in Western Europe the birth

rate lagged 50 to 100 years behind the death rate decline, and substan-

tial rates of natural increase resulted. In France, there is debate if there

was any lag between death rate and birth rate decline, although that

question is obscured by the paucity of eighteenth century demographic

data. But even if a lag occurred, it could not have been long because the

birth rate closely follows the death rate decline such that very small rates

---

[6]R. Easterlin, "Does Human Fertility Adjust to the Environment?,"
American Economic Review, Vol. LXI, no. 2, May 1971, p. 406.

of natural increase are experienced throughout the nineteenth century. It is unclear how the birth rate can be argued to "respond" to the death rate decline when such a short time intervenes between stimulus and response.

Model of Population Pressure for France

As we saw in Chapter I, the demographic transition in France occurs in the nineteenth century and the last half of the eighteenth century. This period is characterized by a declining death rate. In the absence of a similar decline in the birth rate, the rate of natural increase must rise. In the absence of a higher rate of out-migration, the rate of total increase must rise. The literature suggests that this faster population growth puts pressure on the environment. How much population pressure is created depends on the ability of the environment to absorb the larger population. If all the population increase can be absorbed, then there is no population pressure.

During the time of the demographic transition, France is predominantly rural and agricultural. The ability of a primarily agricultural economy to absorb population growth is basically determined by the opportunities for agricultural expansion. The fact that France has been farmed for many centuries and had its population spread out even into inhospitable mountain regions would suggest that the nation might not easily absorb further population increases.

The model of population developed here builds on Friedlander's analysis. The birth rate is taken to be a function not only of the death rate and non-agricultural opportunities, but a function of agricultural opportunities as well. If families can easily support extra children, there will be less pressure to reduce fertility. Pressure on fertility would presumably remain, however, because expansion of agriculture would undoubtedly require more work, if not greater expense.

The mechanism by which the population pressure operates on fertility may be through employment opportunities, as Friedlander assumes. But Kingsley Davis suggests that the impact of population pressure may also be on family consumption levels. While Davis discounts this second impact for agricultural areas in industrializing countries, it would seem to be relevant where opportunities for agricultural expansion may be small. It may even be anticipated that agricultural opportunities for expansion may be more important than non-agricultural opportunities in maintaining consumption levels. It may be harder for farmers to work outside their accustomed occupation to provide extra income than to expand their present agricultural activities.

Agricultural opportunities should probably be added to non-agricultural opportunities and labor force growth as determinants of net migration. Holding employment opportunities constant, net in-migration should be greater where additions to the labor force are greater. And holding additions to the labor force constant, the pressure for net out-migration should be reduced where employment opportunities are greater in either agricultural or non-agricultural occupations.

Where the impact of non-agricultural opportunities might be expected to be small on the birth rate, however, we may expect its impact to be much greater on net migration. New entrants in the labor market can be expected to enter those occupations which promise the best opportunities. If agricultural opportunities are fairly low throughout the country, and if non-agricultural opportunities are expanding, then they can be expected to enter non-agricultural occupations. We saw in Chapter I that the proportion of the population living from agriculture was declining fairly rapidly throughout the nineteenth century. We may hypothesize that many of the additions to the non-agricultural labor force came from new entrants into the labor force, rather than from the labor force established in farming. To the extent that rural-urban migration and movement out of agricultural occupations are associated, the hypothesis is supported by the well-known fact that rural-urban migrants come disproportionately from men in the age group entering the labor force -- men in their early 20's.[7]

Measures of Opportunities

The measure of agricultural opportunities adopted here is a measure of the availability of cultivable land. The potential for expansion of area

---

[7]U. N., Determinants and Consequences of Population Trends, (New York, 1953), p. 302.

under cultivation is useful in understanding responses to both forms of population pressure dealt with in this chapter. One way of expanding agriculture as a response to larger completed family size is by expanding cultivated area. The availability of cultivable land for new farm sites is important in determining employment opportunities in agriculture.

This measure of land potential was calculated by subtracting cultivated land from total cultivable land, then dividing by cultivable land to get the proportion of cultivable land available for agricultural expansion.[8] Cultivated land includes land under any of 7 cereal crops, potatoes, or vines. The cultivable area is taken as the official estimate of "useful agricultural land" for 1965.[9] According to this measure of land potential, 46.9% of cultivable land was available for expansion of cultivation in France in 1846. In 1821, 52.4% was available for expansion.

The measure is biased upwards by the exclusion from cultivated land of land cultivated in other crops, such as various cash crops, vegetables, and fodder crops from artificial meadows. A more important source of

---

[8]Yasuba (Y. Yasuba, Birth Rates of the White Population of the U.S., 1800-1860 (Baltimore: 1962)) uses a simple density measure as an indicator of the availability of agricultural land for the United States and finds it inversely related to fertility, much as I argue here.

[9]France. I. N. S. E. E., Annuaire Statistique de la France, Vol. 73. (Paris: 1967), pp. 199-200. The static nature of this estimate of cultivable land may introduce a bias in the measure. Expansion of land under urban use or the introduction of new technology such as irrigation might change the number of cultivable hectares over time. No evidence has been found, however, that such changes were quantitatively important.

upward bias is the exclusion from cultivated land of fallow. Land left fallow is only available for expansion of crop cultivation if the rotation system is changed, which would constitute a major technological change.[10] While departmental data of these land uses is generally unavailable, national estimates are available which indicate the extent of the bias.[11] When all other crops are included in cultivated land, but fallow is still excluded, the proportion of useable land available for crop expansion crops to 14.6% for 1821 and 17.1% for 1846. When fallow is excluded from land available for expansion, the proportion of land available for expansion drops to 1.2% for 1781-90 and by 1815-24, over 100% of cultivable land is in use (109.3% to 105.4%, depending on the assumption made about the decline in fallow). By 1846, land use has declined to about 100%. These estimates suggest that, for the nation as a whole, there was no opportunity for agricultural expansion through expansion of land under cultivation, in the absence of a change in rotation systems.

It is much more difficult to construct a measure of non-agricultural opportunities. In an attempt to provide for some rough indicator, the proportion of the population not living from agriculture is used here. As % agriculture falls, more employment is in non-agricultural occupations.

---

[10]The exclusion of fallow from cultivated land raises a serious problem of interpretation. Changes in land potential may reflect either expansion on to new land or a change in the rotation system.

[11]Toutain, op. cit., pp. 214-215.

That increased employment may be suggestive of greater employment possibilities. This indicator leaves much to be desired, but it may serve as a crude approximation in the absence of a better measure.

The Birth Rate Decline as Response to Population Pressure

In the first model, the birth rate is taken as a function of the death rate, land potential (the measure of agricultural opportunities), and % agriculture (the indicator of non-agricultural opportunities). This equation was estimated from observations on 78 departments for two separate time periods: 1815-24 to 1840-49, and 1840-49 to 1865-74. % agriculture proves to be highly insignificant in both periods. The equations estimated without % agriculture are as follows:

$$\text{(1)} \quad \underset{(.0856)}{BR_1} = 1.0652 \overset{(.64)}{\underset{(.0856)}{DR_1}} + .0538 \overset{(.06)}{\underset{(.0147)}{LP_1}} + .2580 \qquad R^2 = .7043$$

$$\text{(2)} \quad BR_2 = 1.0256 \overset{(.40)}{\underset{(.1456)}{DR_2}} + .0524 \overset{(.09)}{\underset{(.0187)}{LP_2}} - .9039 \qquad R^2 = .4921$$

Both independent variables are significant both periods at the .99 level at least. Figures in parentheses under the coefficients are the standard errors. Figures in parentheses over the coefficients are the coefficients of separate determination (the normalized regression coefficient times the simple R), showing the variance attributable to each independent variable. The R^2 between the two independent variables is less than .01 for each period, so their influence on birth rate variability is neither additive nor offsetting. Coefficients greater than 1 for death rates reaffirm the hypothesis that the birth rate is very highly responsive to the death rate. Normalized regression coefficients (which adjust for differences of scale and dispersion) are .2304 and .2387 for land potential for periods 1 and 2 respectively. Thus a 1% change in land potential brings about a 1/4% change in the birth rate. While the birth rate appears much less responsive to land potential than to the death rate, each seems to have an important impact on the birth rate.

The hypothesis that the death rate causes changes in the birth rate is only one of several possible explanations for the observed association between birth and death rates. Other logical possibilities are that the birth rate causes changes in the death rate, or that both birth and death rate changes are caused by a third factor. It might also be possible that the observed association between birth and death rates might only reflect the impact of age structure on the crude rates.

If infant mortality is high enough, a drop in the birth rate will result in a large drop in the death rate because there will be fewer babies born to die before the end of the year. Although estimates of infant mortality are notoriously unreliable, calculations by Bertillon[12] of the probability at birth of reaching age 1 provide the best available estimates. He finds for France as a whole that for the period 1840-9, 16% of children die

---

[12]Bertillon, "France (Démographie)," Encyclopédie Dictionnaire des ciences Médicales, p. 573.

before reaching age 1. For 1857-66, 17.8% die in their first year. A 10%

change in the birth rate, then could bring about a 1.6% to 1.8% change in

the death rate. Even if Bertillon's estimates are seriously under-

estimated, it does not seem possible that the 100% responsiveness be-

tween birth and death rates can be fully accounted for in this manner.

Although it seems highly unlikely that the line of causation may run

from birth rate to death rate, it might still be the case that both birth and

death rates are varying with a third factor. The most commonly selected

third factor is the decline of traditionalism -- sometimes formulated as

rationalism, urbanization, industrialization, and even civilization.[13]

While such concepts are not readily quantified, variables such as %

agriculture, % rural, or % literate might be expected to act as proxies for

such developments. Regressions of birth rates for periods 1 and 2 on %

agriculture and % rural yield highly insignificant relationships, with R^2

of .00 and .01 with % agriculture and -.01 and -.02 with % urban.

The measure of literacy employed is the proportion of conscriptees

for the years 1875-76 who were able to read, write, and count.[14] The

correlation coefficient for % literacy and the birth rate for period 2 is

-.52, implying that the higher the literacy rate the lower the birth rate.

A weaker inverse relationship (R = -.26) also exists between the death

---

[13]U. N., op. cit., Chapter V, especially pp. 77-8.

[14]Bertillon, op. cit., pp. 564-565.

rate and % literacy. This data is consistent with the hypothesis that both

birth and death rates are varying with literacy or another variable closely

associated with literacy. To test which hypothesis is correct, equation

(3) estimates the association between birth and death rates when literacy

is held constant. Because the death rate and % literacy are not completely

independent variables, the assumptions of the regression model are

violated and its results are not exact.

$$
\text{(3)} \quad BR_2 = \underset{(.13318)}{\overset{(.37)}{.96631}} DR_2 - \underset{(.00267)}{\overset{(.20)}{.013013}} \%LIT + 13.391 \qquad R^2 = .57
$$

Both independent variables are significant at well over the .995 level

with t-statistics of 7.26 and 4.88 respectively. Coefficients of separate

determination suggest that the death rate accounts for nearly twice the

variance that literacy does. Normalized regression coefficients of .57

for DR_2 and $-.38$ for %LIT suggest that the impact of the death rate is

stronger than the impact of literacy on the birth rate. Equation (3) sub-

stantiates the hypothesis that the birth rate responds to the death rate

even when literacy is taken into account.

To test for the effect of age-structure on the association between

birth and death rates, an age-adjusted fertility measure, the total marital

fertility rate, is calculated for 1861-9 and regressed against the death

rate. This TMFR is calculated by dividing the birth rate by the number of married women aged 15–50 per thousand of the population.[15]

(4) $\text{FMFR} = .11657 \text{ DR}_2 - .93639$ $R^2 = .32$
           $(.0193)$

With a t-statistic of 6.05 the relationship is significant at better than

.995 level. While the proportion of the variance in fertility explained by

the death rate in period two is not as great when fertility is age-adjusted

(32% compared to 44%), equation (4) does suggest that the association be-

tween birth and death rates is not simply due to the crudity of the rates.

Equation (5) tests if land potential is still significantly related to

fertility when the birth rate is age-adjusted.

           $(.27)$ $(.18)$
(5) $\text{TMFR} = .096663 \text{ DR}_2 + .009791 \text{ LP}_2 - .9038$ $R^2 = .45$
           $(.01808)$ $(.002324)$

T-statistics of 5.35 for DR_2 and 4.21 for LP_2 indicate both variables are

significant at better than .995 levels. They account for 27% and 18%

respectively of the variance in TMFR. The normalized regression co-

efficients of .4726 for DR_2 and .3723 for LP_2 indicate that the death rate

has a stronger impact than land potential on fertility.

It is instructive to view the findings of this section in the light of

---

[15]Ibid.

the literature on the French demographic transition.[16] In summarizing

the literature to 1953, <u>Determinants and Consequences of Population</u>

<u>Trends</u> (hereafter <u>D & C</u>) finds perhaps the most plausible hypothesis for

the unexplained European fertility decline to be in the complex changes

in society of the last two centuries. It recognizes, however, that

attempts to link the fertility decline with any one of those changes, such

as urbanization, have provided inadequate explanations.[17] Perhaps the

most important work taking this viewpoint is Leroy-Beaulieu, <u>Question de</u>

<u>la Population</u> who argues that 'civilization' is responsible for the unique

French fertility decline. He includes under 'civilization' such factors as

the decline in income from children accompanying the movement out of

agriculture, the spread of education, democratic ideals, personal ambition,

and a taste for luxuries.[18] It is unclear, however, how such a complex

set of changes could account for the birth rate decline when no clear

---

[16]For a discussion of the literature on the causes of fertility declines
throughout the world, see U. N., <u>op. cit.</u>, Chapter V, "Economic and
Social Factors Affecting Fertility," pp. 71-97. For a review and
classification of literature specifically on the French fertility decline,
see J. Spengler, <u>France Faces Depopulation</u>, Ch. VII, "French Explanations of the Causes of the Decline in Natality," pp. 135-174. Probably
the classic work on the French demographic transition is P. Aries,
<u>Histoire des Populations Francaises</u> (Paris: Éditions Self, 1948).

[17]U. N., <u>op. cit.</u>, p. 77.

[18]P. Leroy-Beaulieu, <u>La Question de la Population</u> (Paris:
Librairie Félix Alcan, 1913), p. 220.

connection can be established to any one of the constituent parts. If

growing literacy is taken as part of the civilizing process, the evidence

in this section suggests that even when civilization is allowed for, the

birth rate still responds to the death rate.

The hypothesis that the birth rate falls in response to the death rate

is given less sympathetic treatment in D & C. In particular, the

hypothesis that the decline in infant mortality allowed the birth rate to

fall because families needed to have fewer additional children to achieve

a desired family size is rejected for France:

> "It has been pointed out, however, that, at least for
> France, the infant mortality reduction could not have
> been responsible for the initial spread of family
> limitation because the decline of the death and birth
> rates occurred as the same time. [19]

The more recent findings of Louis Henry cited in Chapter I, however, cast

doubt on the assertion that birth and death rates fell at the same time in

France. Further, if families actually wait for one child to die before

conceiving another, then a decline in infant mortality can be expected to

bring about an immediate decline in the birth rate through this decline in

replacement fertility.

More recently, Étienne van de Walle has been using more refined

fertility measures to study to French demographic transition. He argues

that the reduction of high levels of mortality is a necessary prerequisite

---

[19]U. N., op. cit., p. 81.

115

for a decline in the birth rate.[20] He does not deal with the possible impact of the death rate on the birth rate, however, because of the unavailability and unreliability of infant mortality data.[21] It is not clear, though, why he does not use the readily available crude death rate data.

Van de Walle finds[22] that age at marriage was very high in France at the start of the demographic transition. For some unexplained reason, probably reflecting changing values, the age at marriage began to fall, probably at about the same time as the death rate decline. He sees the lower age at marriage as putting the same kind of pressure on the family to reduce their fertility as hypothesized in this chapter. He argues that the small family ideal already existed in France. The result is that family limitation measures are adopted to maintain small families in the face of the earlier age at marriage. In the light of his discussion it would be interesting to extend the analysis of this chapter to test the hypothesis that the birth rate decline is a response to the pressures brought about by declining age at marriage as well as a declining death rate and differential opportunities for agricultural expansion.

Van de Walle further argues[23] that the small family ideal may be

---

[20]E. van de Walle, "Demographic Transition in France," mimeo, p. 15.

[21]Ibid., p. 12.

[22]E. van de Walle, "Marriage and Marital Fertility," Daedalus, Spring, 1968, vol. 97, no. 2, pp. 486-501.

[23]E. van de Walle, op. cit., p. 14.

related to cultural differences, diffusing more rapidly among people of the same culture than between cultures. He finds the regional pattern in the timing of the fertility decline crudely associated with the location of French dialects, and associated to a lesser extent with differences in literacy. Thus it may be the case for the analysis in this chapter that literacy stands for the spread of the small family ideal among different subcultures in France.

Migration as Response to Population Pressure

In the second model, net migration is taken as a function of potential labor force growth, agricultural opportunities, and non-agricultural opportunities. The rate of natural increase, lagged 20 years in period 1 and 25 years in period 2, is used as the indicator of potential labor force growth. It should be recognized that this indicator may be weakened by departmental differences in mortality or migration under age 20-25, allowing two departments with the same lagged rate of natural increase to have different rates of potential labor force growth. Land potential and % agriculture are taken as indicators of agricultural and non-agricultural opportunities respectively. When this equation is estimated, land potential is insignificant; in fact, in the numerous other equations estimated, land potential never enters as significant. The equations estimated without land potential are as follows:

$$\text{(6)} \quad RNM_1 = \overset{(.28)}{-0.0726} \%AG - \overset{(.08)}{0.2297} RNI_0 + 5.0264 \qquad R^2 = .3545$$
$$\underset{(.0129)}{} \qquad \underset{(.0832)}{}$$

$$\text{(7)} \quad RNM_2 = \overset{(.30)}{-0.1003} \%AG - \overset{(.13)}{0.3802} RNI_1 + 5.7139 \qquad R^2 = .4314$$
$$\underset{(.0166)}{} \qquad \underset{(.1005)}{}$$

Both independent variables are significant both periods at the .995 level

at least. Normalized regression coefficients are .5196 and .5719 for

%AG and .2566 and .3315 for lagged RNI. The R^2 between the two in-

dependent variables is less than .01 for both periods.

A variety of other equations were estimated to test out the impact of

a variety of other economic factors on the components of the rate of total

increase. Variables tried included growth in hectares, growth in yields,

growth in total production, and a density measure (rural population/

useable agricultural land). None of these variables proved to be con-

sistently related to any of the demographic variables.

Table I summarizes the relationships for both periods found between

these four economic variables and the demographic variables.

While these tests are inconclusive because of the problem of low

dispersion in the demographic magnitudes, there is certainly no evidence

to suggest that conditions in agriculture had a signficant impact on

demographic magnitudes beyond the impact of land potential on the birth

rate.

One other hypothesis of demographic effects of economic change

which seemed of interest is the relationship between the death rate and

TABLE I

Economic-Demographic Interrelations: R^2

Period 1 (1820-1845)

	GH_1	GY_1	GP_1	RP/U_1
BR	.01	.00	.01	.00
DR	.00	.00	.00	.00
RNI	.03	.00	.05	.00
RNM	.01	.01	.02	.01
RTI	.07	.01	.12	.00

Period 2 (1845-1870)

	GH_2	GY_2	GP_2	RP/U_2
BR	.08	.04	.00	.02
DR	.08	.00	.00	.00
RNI	.02	.01	.00	.00
RNM	.00	.01	.00	.00
RTI	.02	.00	.00	.00

GH = growth in cultivated hectares

GP = growth in production

RP/U = rural population per useable (cultivable) hectare

per capita agricultural production. According to the Malthusian argument,
lower levels of per capita output should cause higher levels of death
rates. Using the production data for the four most important cereal
crops, plus potatoes, the following regression equation was estimated
for 78 departments for the period 1820-45:

$$(9) \qquad DR_1 = -0.13147 \, PCPR + 24.695 \qquad\qquad\qquad R^2 = .02$$
$$(.11886)$$

The relation is insignificant at even the 90% level (t-statistic of 1.11).
To allow for departmental differences in the importance of crops, the
measure of per capita production was expanded to include 7 cereal crops
plus potatoes. The resulting relationship was still insignificant (the
t-statistic reached only 1.15). To test the effect of excluding wine production, the 9 departments with 50,000 or more hectares under wine were
excluded from the analysis. The resulting t-statistic of 1.20 is still
highly insignificant. It is possible that the exclusion of other crops,
the indirect estimation of animal production, or the assumption of no
interdepartmental trade may obscure a significant impact of differentials
in per capita consumption on death rate differentials, but the evidence
presented here does not support the hypothesis.

Implications for the Model of Population Pressure

Friedlander finds that the relative importance of birth rate and net
migration responses are determined by the extent of non-agricultural
opportunities. High non-agricultural opportunities lead to a net migration

response; low non-agricultural opportunities lead to a birth rate response. His analysis suggests that an inverse relationship should exist between the birth rate and the rate of net migration. Tests for this inverse relationship for the departments of France find no statistically significant relationship for either period (R^2's are .00 and .04).

One difficulty with Friedlander's model may be that he ignores the impact of agricultural opportunities. With greater agricultural opportunities, there should be less pressure to reduce birth rates. With exceedingly low opportunities for expansion of cultivated land in France, we would anticipate that the birth rate response to the death rate would be great, and the evidence presented here shows that it was very great indeed.

More importantly, Friedlander's discussion suffers from his failure to deal with more than the employment impact of population pressure. The evidence for France suggests that the consumption impact of population pressure may be more important for determining the strength of the birth rate response. When completed family size increases, the immediate pressure is on the consumption level of the family. Response to that pressure should depend on the possibilities for raising income levels to retain living standards. In agricultural areas, these possibilities are influenced greatly by the availability of land for expansion of cultivation. In France where land potential is so low, we would expect the birth rate to be very sensitive to the death rate, as it is. It is not the absolute rate

of population growth (the height of the rate of natural increase) that determines the extent of population pressure, but rather population growth
relative to the environment. Relatively slow population growth in France
leads to great population pressure on the birth rate precisely because of
the lack of opportunities for agricultural expansion through extension of
cultivated area.

The employment impact of population pressure should affect the birth
rate only through anticipated difficulties with inheritance. While Davis
argues that this inheritance consideration is paramount, the insignificance
of non-agricultural opportunities in determining the birth rate suggests
that the employment impact of population pressure on the birth rate was of
lesser importance in France. Yasuba and Easterlin both find for the
United States that the rural fertility decline seems closely related to the
decline in availability of land for agricultural expansion, although they
too argue in terms of the employment impact of population pressure.

Net migration in France seems quite low in the nineteenth century,
with means of -0.09 and -1.49 for the two periods for the agricultural
departments. Seen in relation to levels of the rates of natural increase,
however, migration appears more formidable in period 2. Mean rates of
net migration are found to be strongly related to non-agricultural opportunities, and insignificantly related to agricultural opportunities. These

relationships may be due to the fact that agricultural opportunities are so low nationally and non-agricultural opportunities were expanding. Nevertheless, it is somewhat surprising that agricultural opportunities are significantly related to the birth rate, but are unrelated to the rate of net migration.

The speed of the birth rate response in France becomes less of an anomalie when viewed in the context of the population pressure model developed here. With agricultural opportunities most limited, the impact of population pressure on consumption could be expected to lead to a more immediate birth rate response than if population pressure is seen as working through employment opportunities. Anticipation of employment difficulties in 20 years can not have the immediacy of present pressure on consumption levels.

It is also easier to understand the speed of the French birth rate response when the speed of the death rate decline is recognized. With a death rate falling much slower than in underdeveloped countries since World War II, for example, a lag of the same number of years in the birth rate response leads to much lower gap between birth and death rates.

It is also possible that replacement fertility was a relatively high proportion of total fertility in France. In that case, a decline in the death rate could be expected to be accompanied almost immediately by a birth rate decline. In the absence of evidence, this explanation must remain pure speculation.

Caution must be exercised in attempting to apply the findings for France to other countries. No attempt is made in this chapter to account for the existence of both a birth rate response and a migration response to population pressure. It may be that in another country, response to population pressure might take only one of these forms, or another form altogether. Further, no attempt is made to account for the relative magnitudes of birth rate and migration responses. Even if both responses occur in another country, their relative magnitudes may be quite different.

Conclusion

This chapter develops and tests a model of population pressure for nineteenth century France.

The fundamental notion underlying the concept of population pressure is that population adjusts to its environment. As the death rate declines, especially through declines in infant mortality, completed family size increases. As completed family size gets larger than desired family size, population pressure develops. This pressure may take one of two forms.

First, the family experiences downward pressure on its consumption levels. The response to this pressure is to reduce fertility. The amount of pressure is determined by the opportunities to increase income, and thus to maintain consumption levels. In agricultural areas, such opportunities would generally entail expanding agriculture. It is possible that if opportunities for agricultural expansion are sufficiently great, no pressure will be felt, and no reduction in fertility will result.

Second, population pressure may operate on employment opportunities. As children grow up and prepare to enter the labor market, they might respond to reduced employment opportunities by migration. The pressure on them to migrate is determined both by the number of new entrants into the labor market, but also by the extent of employment opportunities. In a country where agricultural opportunities are shrinking and non-agricultural opportunities are expanding, we would expect that net migration would be primarily determined by the number of new entrants into the labor force, and the extent of non-agricultural employment opportunities.

The evidence presented in this chapter suggests that the birth rate responded with great sensitivity to the death rate, although the birth rate was higher in areas with greater agricultural opportunities. The exceedingly low possibilities for expansion of agriculture would lead us to expect that the birth rate would be highly responsive to the death rate.

Net migration is found to be significantly associated with both potential labor force growth and non-agricultural opportunities, as the model predicts.

Growth of production, or growth in its components of hectares and yields, does not have any significant impact on demographic behavior. This lack of association may possibly be due to the lack of important variations in most of the demographic variables.

The suggestion is made that the reason the birth rate so closely parallels the death rate in France is that the lack of possibilities for agricultural expansion forced an unusually rapid birth rate response to changes in the death rate. Most models of population pressure which operate through the pressure on employment opportunities are unable to explain such a rapid birth rate response.

CHAPTER IV

THE ROLE OF DEMOGRAPHIC CHANGE IN AGRICULTURAL

DEVELOPMENT IN NINETEENTH CENTURY FRANCE

Introduction

In Chapter III we saw that both the birth rate and the rate of natural

increase responded to population pressure. The pressure came about

because a decline in the death rate resulted in an increase in the rate of

natural increase. This faster natural population growth brought at least

two kinds of pressure. First, with declining infant mortality, population

growth means a larger completed family size. This larger family implies

a strain on the consumption levels of the family. Second, as these

additional children grow up and begin to look for employment, pressure

on employment opportunities results. French families apparently responded

to the pressure on family consumption by lowering the birth rate, but where

there were greater opportunities for agricultural expansion there seems to

have been less pressure on the birth rate. The response of young adults

to pressure on employment opportunities was to out-migrate, especially

where non-agricultural employment opportunities were scarce. The mild

impact of agricultural opportunities on the birth rate response, and the

lack of their impact on net migration seems to be due to the fact that for

the nation as a whole, there was no additional land available for

126

agricultural expansion.

This chapter extends the model of population pressure to find whether there were economic responses to demographic change. In particular, it explores the effect of the rate of natural increase on growth in land and labor inputs and growth in yields.

The Land Input

If population pressure on the birth rate was as great as Chapter III indicates, then we would expect higher rates of natural increase would be associated with greater hectare growth. Where the possibilities of land expansion are less, however, we would expect the relationship between growth in hectares and natural increase to be weaker.

There are at least two possible impacts of this population pressure on growth in the land input. The consumption impact of population pressure would bring immediate pressure for agricultural expansion. The employment impact would come with lag. Current rate of natural increase and lagged rate of natural increase respectively are used as indicators of these forms of population pressure.

When growth in hectares is taken as a function of land potential, and either current or lagged natural increase, the rate of natural increase is insignificant. The results of the estimated relationship between hectare growth and land potential are given below.

(1) $\quad GH_1 = 0.5028 \, LP_1 - 5.5433 \qquad\qquad R^2 = .1117$
$\qquad\qquad (.1626)$

(2) $GH_2 = 0.2841 \ LP_2 - 8.0536$ $R^2 = .0986$
        (.0985)

Equations (1) and (2) refer to the periods 1815-24 to 1840-49 and 1840-

49 to 1865-74 respectively. Both coefficients are significant at better

than the .999 level. Because there is some multicollinearity between

land potential and natural increase, the regressions were also run without

land potential. Even in the 2 variable regressions, however, hectare

growth was not significantly related to either current or lagged rate of

natural increase.

It is still possible that population pressure is a common factor in all

departments leading to expansion of hectares, with the amount of expan-

sion determined by land potential. The low variability of natural in-

crease between departments may preclude its observed impact on

differential growth in hectares. Yet natural increase may still help

determine the overall level of hectare growth, with its impact hidden in

the constant term of equations (1) and (2).

It is also possible that the reason population pressure does not seem

to have an impact on hectare growth is that the growth in hectares is

biased. As the discussion in Chapter II indicated, the hectares of only

5 crops are included in this measure. The growth in hectares of those 5

crops may reflect changes in crop composition as well as expansion of

cultivated area. Area under crops not included may decline, while total

area cultivated remains constant. The further bias associated with not

using the 3 additional cereal crops was discounted in the national analysis because growth in area under those crops was roughly the same as for the 5 crop average. In these regressions, where departmental observations are used, this further bias may be more important. For example, departments may be expanding cultivation of their major crops, at the expense of other crops. Departments specializing in crops not covered might increase cultivation in cereals and potatoes as fast as the rest of France, yet because the area under included crops is declining, the measured growth in those departments will be less.

This possible bias was partly corrected for the period 1815-24 to 1840-49 by including the three excluded cereal crops -- mixed wheat and rye, buckwheat, and corn and millet -- in the measure of hectare growth. There are other crops, noteably wine, cash crops like silkworms and flax, and various fodder crops, which are still not included.

When this revised estimate of hectare growth is taken as a function of either lagged or current natural increase, and land potential, natural increase is still insignificant. Because of the multicollinearity between natural increase and land potential (r^2 = .15 for lagged and r^2 = .16 for current natural increase), revised growth in hectares is taken as a function of natural increase alone. The results of these regressions are given below.

(3) $\quad RGH_1 = 2.3882 \, RNI_1 + 6.8432 \qquad\qquad\qquad R^2 = .0582$
$\qquad\qquad (1.101)$

(4) $\quad RGH_1 = 2.4689 \, RNI_0 + 5.2039 \qquad\qquad\qquad R^2 = .0556$
$\qquad\qquad (1.1671)$

Both coefficients are significant at the .95 significance level.

The direction of the causation in equations (3) and (4) is unclear, however. It might be the case that greater growth in hectares represents improving consumption which, in Malthusian fashion, prompts higher birth rates and thus greater rates of natural increase. In view of the uniformly falling birth rates throughout France, such a hypothesis seems unlikely. A regression was run testing for a relationship between the level of the birth rate and the revised estimate of the growth in hectares for the period 1815-24 to 1840-49. The relationship proved highly insignificant.

The inter-correlation between RNI and land potential suggests that equations (3) and (4) should not be taken as unqualified support for the hypothesis that hectare growth is the result of population pressure. The conclusion of this section must be, therefore, that the data do not support this hypothesis. However, the results are sufficiently ambiguous to leave the question open. Further research on land use is needed before the question can be resolved.

The Labor Input

The growth in the potential labor force, as we may think of the lagged rate of natural increase, does not have a clear impact on the growth in hectares. Yet for the regions, at least, the man/land ratio is fairly constant over time. It may be that the growth in hectares determines the demand for labor, to the extent that fixed proportions of land and labor are needed in agriculture prior to important mechanization. The

estimator of the agricultural labor force employed in Chapter II is a

measure of rural population. The hypothesis is that the growth in rural

population is a function of the growth in hectares. The results of test-

ing for this relationship are given below for period 1. Period 2 produced

insignificant results, with a t-statistic of 1.85.

(5) GRP_1 = 0.8293 GH_1 + 9.7729 R^2 = .0515
               (.4082)

The coefficient is barely significant at the .95 level (t-statistic of 2.03).

The relationship was retested using the revised estimate of growth in

hectares:

(6) GRP_1 = 0.79725 RGH_1 + 11.297 R^2 = .0703
               (0.33256)

The coefficient is still only significant at the .95 level, but the t-statistic

is up to 2.40.

There does seem to be some mixed evidence that growth in hectares

has an influence on the growth in the actual labor force, possibly

through the demand for labor.

This result suggests a more general model. An increase in the rate

of natural increase results, with a lag, in the growth in the labor force.

The greater the non-agricultural employment opportunities available within

a region, the less out-migration there will be. The greater the opportun-

ities for employment in agriculture, the more the growth in agricultural

labor force.

The first part of the model was tested in Chapter III and found to be consistent with the data.

In the second part, both growth in hectares and land potential are tried as indicators of agricultural employment opportunities. When growth in rural population is taken as a function of lagged rate of natural increase and land potential or either growth in hectares or revised growth in hectares, the indicator of agricultural employment opportunities is insignificant. The relationships between growth in actual labor force (rural population) and growth in potential labor force (lagged rate of natural increase) for both periods are as follows:

$$(7) \qquad GRP_1 \;=\; 1.9311 \; RNI_0 + 2.8581 \qquad\qquad\qquad R^2 = .3762$$
$$(.2852)$$

$$(8) \qquad GRP_2 \;=\; 1.0888 \; RNI_1 + 7.4921 \qquad\qquad\qquad R^2 = .0846$$
$$(.41077)$$

In period 2 the coefficient is barely significant at the .99 level, while in period 1 it is significant at least at the .9995 level.

The data do not support the second part of the model. In general, in this section, there is some evidence that actual labor force growth is influenced by the growth in hectares, but there is no evidence to support extensions of the population pressure model. Growth in both land and labor inputs seem to depend primarily on the measures of their potential for growth.

Growth in Yields

Population pressure creates the need to expand production. Where there is little opportunity for hectare growth, that pressure might bring about productivity increases. The pressure might operate through family consumption levels, bringing productivity changes fairly rapidly. Or it might operate through employment. In more general terms, either too much or too little labor could bring pressure for technological change. One possibility is that labor supply might grow faster than labor demand, creating surplus labor and lending impetus to the introduction of a labor-using technology, such as mixed farming. The other possibility is that labor demand grows faster than labor supply, leading to labor shortages and the introduction of a labor-saving technology, such as mechanization.

Population pressure on the birth rate seems clear enough in nineteenth century France, but the birth rate response is so rapid and so complete that it is not necessarily the case that surplus labor resulted. Out-migration further relieved the pressure on employment opportunities. In fact, the apparent lack of response of the rate of net migration to employment opportunities in agriculture suggests that any residual population pressure would be small. This a priori evidence for the existence of either excess demand or supply of labor is unclear.

The discussion in the literature over surplus labor and labor shortages seems to revolve around a debate over the existence of landless labor. It is quite clear that some authors feel that there was landless labor, which was the product of excess labor supply, resulting from popu-

lation pressure. This position is most clearly stated by Gordon Wright:

> ...a large proportion of peasants remained landless
> throughout the nineteenth century. [1]

> ...the landless farm population probably continued to
> exceed the number of landowners in the half-century that
> followed the revolution. If there was any dominant trend
> during this period, it was toward a steadily increasing
> subdivision of the soil. The number of farms in operation
> reached a peak of about 3.5 million in the 1880's. The
> cause seems to have been, quite simply, the growing
> pressure of population on the land. France's rural popu-
> lation reached its all-time peak in the late 1840's, and
> even the drift to the cities that set in thereafter did not
> do much to relieve the pressure until the end of the
> century. Most of the peasantry, therefore, remained on
> a marginal standard that permitted at best only slight and
> sporadic improvement in living conditions and agricultural
> techniques. [2]

In referring to the state of French agriculture in 1815, Clough agrees

that the number of small holdings has increased, insisting on the exis-

tence of a "large, landless agricultural proletariat." [3] And Augé-Laribé

asserts that it was the countryside which, during the first half of the

nineteenth century, chased its out-migration to the towns. He argues

that most of those out-migrating were landless labor -- manual laborers

---

[1]Gordon Wright, Rural Revolution in France: The Peasantry in Twentieth Century, 1964, p. 3.

[2]Ibid., p. 6.

[3]Clough, op. cit., p. 91.

out of work, either seasonally or permanently.[4]

Clapham however, is emphatic about the lack of landless labor.

> In reference to the early nineteenth century, it was pointed out that old France did not contain a regular class of landless labourers, and that the Revolution did nothing to produce such a class. The peasant's son inherited the holding. The day laborer saved and rented a bit of land. The peasant without land enough put in a short day's work for a wage...and tended his own patch in the evenings. There were of course everywhere some landless individuals...but the real rural labouring class, the proletariat, the 'wage slaves' of Marxian economics, did not exist. And the partial industrializing and commercializing, in the later nineteenth century, had not produced such a class, in spite of assertions to the contrary.[5]

It is difficult to evaluate the weight of this literary evidence. Clapham does use whatever empirical evidence he can uncover in establishing his positions, while both Wright and Clough rely more heavily on secondary, non-empirical sources. In general, the debate seems to be over the existence of a labor surplus, and not a labor shortage, and it seems to be as yet unresolved.

The empirical evidence nationally is not much more revealing.

While Figures 1 and 2 in Chapter II present the national trends in population and labor force, and in output and cultivated land, little can be said of a definite nature about either supply or demand for labor. In the period of 50 to 75 years before 1820, population has been growing at

---

[4]Augé-Laribé, op. cit., pp. 82-83.

[5]Clapham, op. cit., p. 162.

its most rapid rate since 1700. If population is any indicator of the level of demand for agricultural production, and hence agricultural labor, then the period preceding the most rapid growth in agriculture is characterized by growing labor demand. However, with something like a 20 year lag, growth in population begets growth in the labor force. And while the proportion of the labor force in agriculture was probably declining slowly since the latter part of the eighteenth century, the agricultural labor force grows almost as fast as population from 1775 to 1850. Thus the period before 1820 may be considered to see growth in both demand and supply of labor.

It might be the case that if labor does not grow as rapidly as other inputs, a labor shortage may exist; however, the labor force per cultivated hectare is almost constant from 1775 to 1820. It might also be the case that if the per capita production declines that the insufficient growth in production might be due to a labor shortage; however, per capita production is constant from 1775 to 1820. In general, the evidence gleaned from the national trends in population and agriculture indicate that while the period preceding the rapid growth in agriculture does include some of the most rapid population growth in modern French history, no suggestion can be found for either labor scarcity or labor surplus.

While no evidence can be found on the national level for labor scarcity or surplus, it is possible that it might be found on the regional level. Or it might be found that other demographic changes are

influencing agriculture. In Chapter I a regional classification is devised
which brings out most sharply what differential demographic patterns
exist in France in each of the components of the rate of total increase.
One of the important conclusions of Chapter II, however, is that even
when differentials in demographic behavior are brought out most clearly,
the overall picture is one of regional uniformity: regional demographic
differentials are not great when a few major urban centers are excluded.
This demographic uniformity makes it difficult to detect the impact of
demographic factors on agriculture by observing if the regional classification which best brings out demographic differentials also brings out any
consistent differences in agricultural patterns. The expectation would be
that if labor scarcity exists in France in the early nineteenth century,
regions with the lowest natural increase (regions A) would exhibit the
most labor scarcity, so that if labor scarcity induces new technology and
more production, regions A would tend to have higher growth in production
than regions B. In fact, when this regional classification is employed in
Chapter I, it shows regional uniformity in replicating the national patterns.
While some regional agricultural variations from the national pattern exist,
they do not conform to demographic differences between regions. Even
taking into account the difficulties raised by the lack of wide regional
demographic variation, the conclusion must be that no evidence exists in
the regional data for any effect of demographic change on economic
behavior.

Even though national trends and regional differentials do not indicate any impact of demographic change on developments in agriculture, it may be that with the greater variations found in the departmental data and the large number of observations it may be possible to statistically uncover relationships not observable at a more aggregated level.

Several regressions were run to test the effect of population pressure on growth in yields. Growth in yields was taken as a function of potential labor force growth and agricultural opportunities (land potential), actual labor force growth (growth in rural population), and actual labor force growth and agricultural opportunities. These were run for both periods. The only significant (inverse) relationship uncovered was between growth in yields and land potential, and that in period 2 (1840-49 to 1865-74) only.

The evidence presented in this section lends no support to the hypothesis that population pressure had any impact on the growth in yields.

Conclusion

The general conclusion reached in this chapter is that population pressure did not have much impact on developments in agriculture, which is perhaps not so surprising when one considers the relatively low rates of population growth.

Growth in land inputs does have some association with lagged natural increase, but not when land potential is held constant. It may be, owever, that the impact of lagged natural increase is obscured by its low

ariance. Given the evidence presented here, the best we can say is

1at hectares under cultivation grew more where there was more oppor-

1nity for them to grow.

There seems to be some mixed evidence that growth in hectares helped

etermine the growth in the demand for labor, and thus the agricultural

bor force.

Productivity increases were apparently quite independent of demo-

aphic developments. Because of the importance of these productivity

1creases in accounting for the rapid and unexpected growth in agricul-

ral production before mid-century, the next chapter explores in a pre-

minary fashion the possible sources of that productivity increase.

CHAPTER V

THE PRODUCTIVITY INCREASE IN NINETEENTH

CENTURY FRENCH AGRICULTURE

Chapter II presented evidence that French agricultural production grew at an unprecedented rate in the period from 1815 to 1870. While inputs of both land and labor grew during this period, productivity increases of both land and labor accounted for much of the growth in output. This chapter examines the hypothesis of Chapter II that the development of mixed farming may account for this growth in agriculture. It traces the possible diffusion of mixed farming through France. The discussions in this chapter are meant to be purely exploratory, following up the surprising developments in agricultural productivity uncovered in Chapter II and suggesting further lines of research.

The Source of the Productivity Increase

Most of the suggestions in the literature accounting for rapid growth in nineteenth century French agriculture point to developments that took place after midcentury, when the agricultural revolution is generally understood to have taken place. The developments included expansion of markets through the building of railroads, use of artificial fertilizer, mechanization, scientific breeding, and the growth of mixed farming. Most of the rapid growth in agriculture, however, takes place before

midcentury, leaving the explanation of most of the agricultural revolution
o earlier developments.

It was found in Chapter II (page 90) that the declines in fallow and
growth in artificial meadows which signal the change to mixed farming
were at least as great before midcentury as after. This raised the
possibility that the development of mixed farming might underlie the growth
n agriculture.

Prior to the introduction of mixed farming, rotation systems required
that large areas of good cropland lie fallow. Under the old 2 field system,
ne field would be planted with a staple cereal crop such as wheat or rye
nd the other field would remain fallow or unused. The next year the use
f the two fields would be reversed, with the former fallow field now re-
lenished and ready to grow grain, and the former grain field exhausted
nd in need of rest. Farm animals were grazed on marginal land used as
asture, and during the winter they were fed whatever grass was mowed
rom (natural) meadows. However, meadows were few because all good
and was needed for crops for human food, especially when half the good
and lay fallow. Consequently animals were typically thin and tired.

Naturally there were variants of this 2 field system. One found in
southern France was the 4 field 2 crop system. Here 2 fields alternated
etween fallow and human crops such as wheat or rye, and the other 2
elds alternated between fallow and animal feed crops such as oats or
arley. The two sets of fields might then switch uses so that one field

would go through a cycle of wheat, fallow, oats, and fallow every four

years.

In the North of France, a more efficient 3 field system was prevalent.

Here a typical field would go through a cycle of wheat or rye, oats or

barley, and fallow for the third year. One third instead of one half of

crop land lay fallow under this system.

Such was the state of French agriculture at least up through 1750.

In the second half of the eighteenth century, progressive French farmers

or agronomes began to receive reports of new rotation systems being used

in England. Similar rotation systems had actually been used in Flanders

to the north of France for several centuries and were known to farmers in

the extreme North of France. The most famous of these English rotation

systems was the Norfolk rotation where 4 different crops might be rotated

without fallow. A typical field under this rotation might be planted with

winter grain, turnips, spring grain, and legumes in a four year period.

When the field was planted with a leguminous (grass) crop as part of a

rotation system, it was called an "artificial meadow." The advantages

of this system were several. First, by avoiding fallow, all good

agricultural land could be cultivated each year. Second, legumes such

as clover added nitrogen to the soil needed by the grain crops, raising

grain yields. Third, the turnips and legumes could be harvested and

used for winter feed for the farm animals. Fourth, the more complete use

of good agricultural land allowed more land to be used as natural (or permanent) meadows, providing more animal feed. The larger and more numerous animals had several uses. They could be slaughtered, improving both quantity and quality of human diet. They could be used as motive power for machinery which enabled a farmer to extend the area under cultivation. And the manure created by the animals during the winter could be collected (especially if they were stall fed) and used as natural fertilizer on the fields, also raising grain yields. This entire "bundle" of technology is called mixed farming.[1]

During the last half of the eighteenth century, agricultural newspapers and books pressed for the adoption of some form of mixed farming. But change in agriculture comes slowly. Singer, in his history of technology, indicates that the development of the technology accompanying the reduction of fallow and the rise in artificial meadows originated very early in Flanders, spreading there to England, among other countries, but "...the attempt to improve French agricultural techniques was only begun just before the Revolution, and in imitation of what had been achieved in England."[2] By the French Revolution, mixed farming had apparently become prevalent only around Paris and in the extreme North in French Flanders.

---

[1]For a comprehensive discussion of European rotation systems, see B. H. Slicher van Bath, The Agrarian History of Western Europe A.D. 500-1850, London, 1963.

[2]C. Singer, et. al., (eds.), A History of Technology, Vol. III, (England: Oxford, 1957), pp. 12-15.

Table I presents data on the magnitudes of national land use for 7 grain crops, potatoes, artificial meadows, and fallow for the period from 1815 to 1884. It includes the most important crops in the rotation system. In the absence of a direct estimate for 1815-24 the estimate of fallow for 1781-90 is used, on the assumption that the events surrounding the French Revolution and its aftermath and the Napoleonic Wars were sufficiently disruptive to preclude major changes in agricultural technology.

Table I shows that twice as much land was cultivated in the rotation system as was used for fallow. In other words, fallow accounted for roughly one-third (35%) of the land in the rotation system. That proportion of fallow is what would be expected under a 3 field system. It no doubt actually represents a 3 field system primarily in the Center and North, with the 2 field system in the South balancing the systems with little or no fallow in the extreme North. Lack of regional figures on either fallow or artificial meadows make it impossible to check this hypothesis. The proportion of fallow in the rotation system decline greatly during the nineteenth century: from 35% in 1815-24 to 28% in 1835-44, to 21% in 1855-64, and to 15% in 1875-84. Thus during the period of rapid national growth in agriculture fallow declined from better than one field in three to less than one field in five.

It is interesting to note that the decline in fallow is sufficient to explain much of the growth in area under cultivation in the nineteenth century. It explains two thirds of the growth in the period 1815-24 to

TABLE I

Land Use (in millions of hectares)

USE	1815-24	1835-44	1855-64	1875-84 **	CHANGES 1815-21 to 1835-44	1835-44 to 1855-64	1855-64 to 1875-84
Wheat	4.815	5.489	6.698	6.859	+ .674	+1.209	+ .161
Oats	2.531	2.905	3.153	3.501	+ .374	+ .248	+ .348
Rye	2.677	2.679	2.068	1.838	+ .002	- .611	- .230
Barley	1.198	1.289	1.102	1.079	+ .091	- .187	- .023
Mixed wheat and rye	.877	.901	.568	.473	+ .024	- .333	- .095
Buckwheat	.645	.682	.747	.660	+ .037	+ .065	- .087
Maize	.582	.611	.651	.661	+ .029	+ .040	+ .010
Potatoes	.576	.916	1.013	1.249	+ .340	+ .097	+ .236
Artificial meadows	1.400	1.831	3.159 3.095	4.497	+ .431	+1.328 +1.264	+1.338 +1.402
Total Crops	15.301	17.303	19.159 19.095	20.817	+2.002	+1.856 +1.792	+1.658 +1.722
Fallow	8.1*	6.763	5.148	3.644	-1.337	-1.615	-1.504
%Fallow / Total Crops					67%	87% 90%	91% 87%

* 1781-90

** Figures for 7 cereals and potatoes actually for year 1876

Source for fallow and artificial meadows: Toutain, pp. 214-215.
Source for crops: Récoltes des Céreales et des Pommes de Terre 1815-1876.

1835-44, and around 90% from 1835-44 to 1875-84. It may be possible, then, that the introduction of mixed farming may explain much of the growth of the land input as well as the productivity increase. In the absence of regional fallow data, the comparisons of magnitudes of crop area increases and fallow declines must be considered merely suggestive.

The growth in area planted in crops such as oats, grown primarily for animal feed,[3] and the growth in artificial meadows providing fodder crops, suggests that the number of farm animals may have increased significantly. Table IV in Chapter 2 shows potato production growing by 75% and oats production by 63% in the period from 1815-19 to 1860-64. Henri Sée claims that (my translation) "...from 1800 to 1835 the quantity of animals more than doubled...."[4] While this estimate may well be over optimistic, the evidence does suggest important growth in the number of farm animals during the period of rapid national growth in agriculture.

The existence of extensive departmental data for midcentury (1852) from the first complete agricultural census allows us to test cross-sectionally our hypotheses about changes in productivity over time. The census provides departmental data on fallow land, artificial meadows, and manure applied per hectare.

If mixed farming has an important impact on the level of yields,

---

[3]L. Mounier, De l'Agriculture en France, d'apres les Documents Officiels, 1846, p. 361, says oats are eaten almost exclusively by horses.

[4]H. Sée, op. cit., p. 27.

departments with a low proportion of fallow should have higher yields.

The proportion of fallow for 1852 is calculated by dividing fallow hectares

by hectares under 7 cereal crops, potatoes, and artificial meadows. The

results of the regression, using all 85 departments for 1852 to test the

relationship between fallow and yields, are given below.

(1) YL_{52} = -0.096607 % FALL + 18.38 R^2 = .1387
          (.026415)

With a t-statistic of 3.66, the relationship is significant at better than

the .995 level. The relationship is as predicted: the greater the propor-

tion of land fallow, the lower the level of yields.

It is not enough, however, to support the hypothesis that mixed

farming raised yield levels. We would like to know what parts of the

bundle of technology of mixed farming actually bring about the change in

yields. The use of manure, the addition of nitrogen to the soil, or some

other aspect of mixed farming might account for the growth in yields. To

test out how mixed farming raises yields, the level of yields in 1852 is

taken as a function of the proportion of artificial meadows to other crops,

the amount of manure fertilizer used per hectare, and the proportion of

fallow to cultivated land (to catch any residual effects of mixed farming

on yields).

                (.11)   (.10)   (.12)
(2) YL_{52} = .017678 MN/H − .068933 %FALL + .13817 ARTM + 12.167
              (.007716)   (.024738)   (.05035)
                                                        R^2 = .3238

MN/H is significant at the .95 level (t-statistic of 2.29), while %FALL

(2.79) and ARTM (2.77) are significant at the .99 level. The coefficients

of separate determination (in parentheses over the regression coeffi-

cients) show that all three variables share equally in the explanation of

the variance. With normalized regression coefficients of .24, .27, and

.28 respectively, all three have about the same impact on yield levels:

a 4% change in any of the variables is accompanied by about a 1% change

in yields.

Apparently the introduction of mixed farming has an impact on yields

beyond the addition of nitrogen to the soil and the use of manure as

fertilizer. The nature of this third effect on yields is unclear. It might

be that the greater use of farm animals in conjunction with improved farm

implements for soil preparation, seeding, or harvesting might be respon-

sible for the additional effect on yields. The determination of this third

impact of mixed farming must await further research.

This section has shown that major changes in rotation systems took

place in France during the period of rapid national growth. Cross-sectional

data for midcentury show that mixed farming has an important impact on

yields. At least three equally important effects of mixed farming are

isolated: the addition of nitrogen to the soil, the use of manure fertilizer,

and some other effect, as yet undertermined. The decline in fallow with

the rise of mixed farming is also found to be sufficient to explain most of

the growth in land inputs during this period. The implication is that the

introduction of mixed farming may prove to be at the heart of the agricultural revolution in nineteenth century France.

The Diffusion of Mixed Farming

The regional analysis of agricultural trends in Chapter 2 concluded that there were some regional differences in the timing of growth in production. In 1815, the North started with the highest yield levels. The Center of France experienced the fastest growth in output between 1815 and 1870. The primary reason for the faster output growth was faster growth in productivity. The South experienced the slowest growth in production and productivity. Beginning late in this period, and especially in the years after 1870, the South had rapid increases in productivity, catching up to the national average by the 1890's. There is some suggestion from these regional comparisons that growth in productivity began in the North and moved south during the nineteenth century. If an important source of the productivity increase is the introduction of mixed farming, what we are probably observing is the diffusion of the new technology of mixed farming.

Figure 1 shows the level of average yields for 5 cereal crops and potatoes in 1815-19. The extreme northern edge of France has the highest yields. There seem to be three centers of highest productivity in Northern France: the Paris Basin, French Flanders, and the western-most portion of Brittany. If mixed farming is taken as the source of high yields, this geographical configuration is quite predictable. The Paris Basin could be

Figure 1

Yields of 5 Major Crops, 1815-19

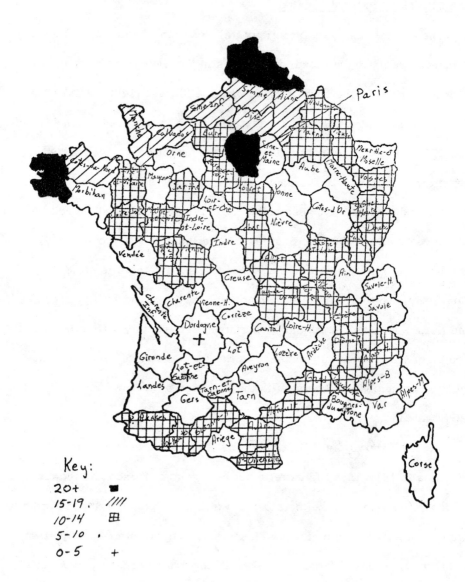

Key:

20+	◼
15-19	////
10-14	⊞
5-10	.
0-5	+

expected to have particularly high yields, no matter their source: the land in the Paris Basin is the most fertile in the nation, and the close proximity of an international urban center would provide ready markets and exposure to the latest technology. This exposure might take the form of displays of new farm equipment or techniques at trade shows or expositions, publication of farm newspapers or magazines, or even greater numbers of travelers who have observed foreign agriculture. French Flanders was once part of Flanders, where mixed farming was introduced as early as the fourteenth century, and has been predominant for several centuries. Brittany, on the other hand, is generally considered one of the most backward parts of France, where yields might be expected to be quite low. However, Brittany is quite close geographically to England, from where the literature says France acquired mixed farming. When Figure 1 is seen as a map of the location of mixed farming, it suggests the hypothesis that the technology of mixed farming came into France through a process of geographical diffusion (farm to nearby farm), modified by diffusion to Paris (city to surrounding farms).

Figure 2 shows the growth in yields from 1815-24 to 1840-49. When it is viewed in conjunction with Figure 1, it provides a picture of the diffusion of high yields, and probably mixed farming. A major region of growth in this period is the line of departments directly south of the highest yields departments of the extreme North in 1815-19. Presumably, mixed farming slowly diffused after it demonstrated its effectiveness in

Figure 2

% Growth in Yields: 1815–24 to 1840–49

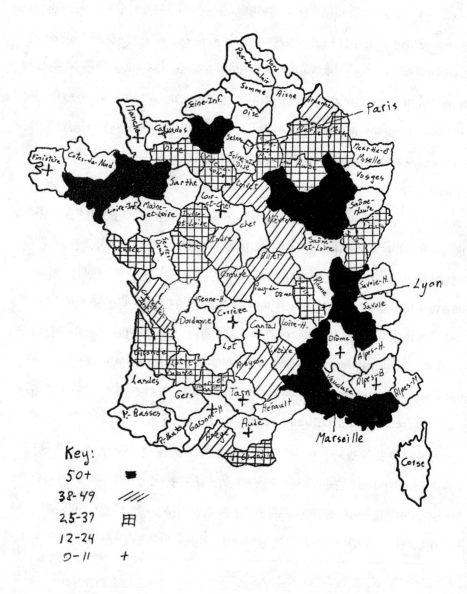

Key:
50+
38-49
25-37
12-24
0-11

the northern-most tier of departments. In discussing the process of geographical diffusion, Clapham speaks of the skillful farmer of Flanders or the plain of Nimes where "...his root crops fattened his beasts and his beasts fattened his land in profitable rotation. The farmers of adjacent departments, now at length copying his methods, made even more progress than he, for they started from a far lower level."[5]

The other major area of rapidly growing yields is the southern coast by Marseille, the second largest city in France, and up the Garonne River to Lyon, the third largest city in France. Every department which had very high yield levels in 1815-19 has very low growth rates in the period 1815-24 to 1840-49. The pattern of geographical diffusion found in Figure 1 is borne out in Figure 2.

Figure 3 shows the yield levels attained by 1840-49. As expected, from the southern diffusion found in preceeding figures, the area of highest yields now encompasses most of the North of France; while rapid growth was enjoyed in the South in the previous quarter century, initial yield levels were so low that only one area near Lyon has yields comparable to the far North.

Growth in yields for the period 1840-49 to 1865-74 shown in Figure 4 is very largely concentrated in the area around Bordeaux, the fourth largest city in France. Some further diffusion from the North is seen as

---

[5]Clapham, op. cit., p. 27.

Figure 3

Yields: 1840-1844 to 1845-1849

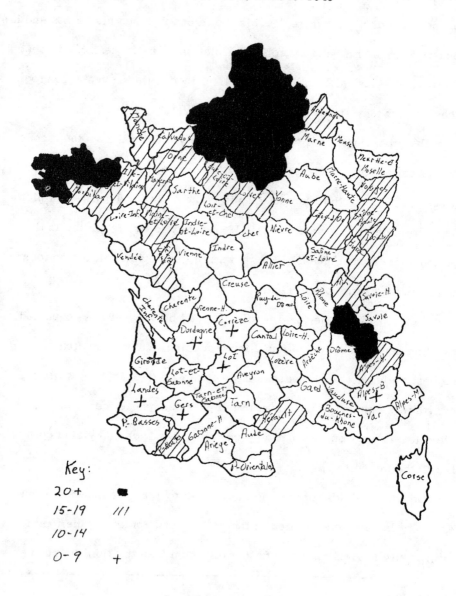

Key:
20+ ■
15-19 ///
10-14
0-9 +

Figure 4

% Growth in Yields: 1840-49 to 1865-74

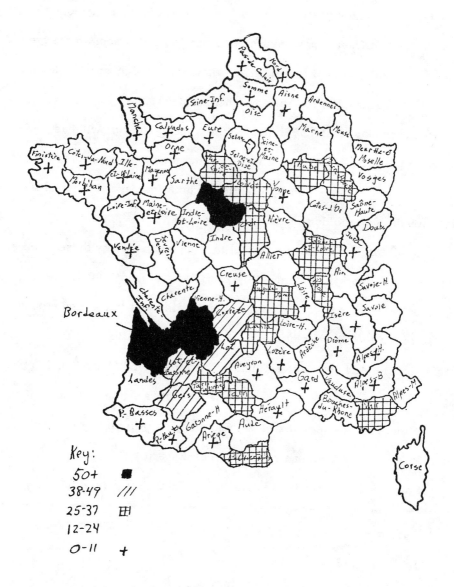

Key:
50+ ■
38-49 ///
25-37 ⊞
12-24
0-11 +

well. Again, the slowest yield growth is found in the areas which had highest yield levels at the start of the period.

Figure 5, which gives the yield levels in 1865-74, brings out an aspect of the diffusion process which is not so clearly seen in the pre-ceeding maps. Figure 5 reveals that, although the highest yield levels are still to be found in the same Northern regions, high yield levels are now found in most areas of France. While spectacular growth has occurred primarily around major urban centers and on the edges of high yield areas, slow steady growth in yields radiating beyond these areas has brought high yields to much of France.

The picture of diffusion of mixed farming suggested by these figures finds some support in Pautard. He asserts that around 1800, little regional variation exists.[6] Then, mixed farming was introduced around Paris, owing to (my translation) "...a happy combination of circumstances: highly fertile land, relative proximity to more evolved Flemish and English agriculture, and nearness to the best centers of research and ideas of the Paris region."[7] He sees that new technology as diffusing very slowly up to midcentury, creating important regional disparities.[8]

If high yields from mixed farming diffused to low yield regions, we

---

[6]Pautard, op. cit., p. 67.

[7]Ibid., p. 118.

[8]Ibid., pp. 67-68.

Figure 5

Yields: 1865-74

Key:

20+	■
15-19	///
10-14	
0-9	+

would expect an inverse relationship between the level of yields at the

beginning of a period and the growth in yields during that period. Equa-

tions 3 and 4 give the estimated relationships for the periods 1815–24 to

1840–49 and 1840–49 to 1865–74.

$$(3) \quad GY_1 = -1.6644 \, IY_1 + 48.5167 \qquad\qquad R^2 = .11$$
$$ (0.5505)$$

$$(4) \quad GY_2 = -2.2739 + 47.2145 \qquad\qquad R^2 = .33$$
$$ (.3707)$$

With t-statistics of 3.02 and 6.13 respectively, both observed inverse

relationships are significant at well over the .99 level, supporting the

pattern observed on the maps.

Conclusion

This chapter presents evidence which suggests that the agricultural

revolution in nineteenth century France may have been largely the product

of the introduction of mixed farming. The decline of fallow which heralds

the initiation of mixed farming can account for much of the growth in the

land input during the period 1815–24 to 1865–74 when the important

agricultural growth took place. Mixed farming is shown to have important

impacts on yields in several ways: through the addition of nitrogen to

soil by the planting of leguminous crops on artificial meadows; through

the use of manure collected from farm animals as natural fertilizer; and

through other unspecified effects, possibly the use of farm animals in

conjunction with improved farm equipment.

The geographical patterns of yields support the view that mixed farming lies behind the productivity increase. The initial areas of high yields are just those areas where mixed farming would be first introduced. The diffusion of mixed farming, or at least the diffusion of high yields, generally takes the form of geographical radiation from areas with high yields. However, fully as important are the jumps in the diffusion process from large city to large city of information on the new technology. During the period under observation, mixed farming jumps from Paris in the North to Marseille and Lyon in the South to Bordeaux in the West -- a movement from the largest city, to the second and third cities, to the fourth largest city.

CONCLUSION

The primary focus of this study is the development of a body of regional economic and demographic data which can be used to study inter-relationships between population growth and agricultural development in nineteenth century France. Much of the study is descriptive, setting out the important national and regional patterns in these data. While a few interesting findings emerge from the exploration of economic-demographic interrelationships using these regional data, the low rates of population growth and the striking uniformity of regional demographic patterns obscure many possible interrelationships. A bi-product of this study is the unexpected finding of rapid agricultural growth in the first half of the nineteenth century.

Against the basic pattern of regional demographic uniformity, some variation may be found. Major urban areas, especially Paris, account for much of what regional variation exists. They exhibit high birth and death rates, low rates of natural increase, high rates of in-mirgration, and high rates of total increase. Outside the major urban areas, greater out-migration is found where there is a higher proportion of the population living from agriculture.

Some significant interrelationships exist between the components of the rate of total increase. Birth rates are strongly associated with both death rates and rates of natural increase. Natural increase and net

160

migration may be interrelated. And the rate of total increase is related to rates of both natural increase and net migration.

While regional demographic data are readily available for the nineteenth century there has been no attempt made to develop regional estimates of agricultural output or inputs before 1860. This study uses official data on production and hectares for major cereal crops and potatoes to develop crude regional estimates of agricultural production and land inputs. An even more crude estimate of labor inputs is constructed using regional figures for total population and population in large towns.

The national agricultural picture is one of rapid agricultural growth between the end of the Napoleonic Wars in 1815 and the Franco-Prussian War in 1870. The primary source of this growth is increases in productivity, although inputs of both land and labor experience some modest growth. The growth in yields is shared by all cereal crops, but not by potatoes. Some important changes in crop composition also occur, with wheat, oats, and potatoes gaining in importance and barley and rye production declining. The changes in crop composition primarily reflect changes in area planted.

Overall, the regions reflect these national patterns. Some regional differences do exist, however. The North starts with the highest levels of output per capita and yields. The Center experiences the most rapid growth in total production and yields, while the South has the slowest growth in the first half of the century. Later in the nineteenth century, however, the South grows rapidly, catching up to national yield averages.

The regional data are used to test a model of population pressure. Briefly, the model asserts that population adjusts to its environment. Falling death rates raise rates of natural increase, putting pressure on a family to either reduce fertility or expand income. The regression results suggest that the birth rate responded with great sensitivity to the death rate, although the response was less where agricultural opportunities, in the form of potential for expansion of cultivated land, were high. The exceedingly low potential for expansion of cultivated land for France as a whole may help explain its unique demographic behavior -- both the early start of the demographic transition, and the low rates of natural increase.

Net migration is significantly associated with both potential labor force and non-agricultural opportunities, as the model of population pressure predicts. The lack of impact of agricultural opportunities on net migration is probably due to the low potential for expansion of cultivation in a time of rising non-agricultural opportunities.

Perhaps because of the completeness of the demographic responses to population pressure, with low growth in population resulting, agricultural developments prove largely independent of population pressure. In particular, the rapid growth in productivity from 1815-1870 appears to be independent of demographic change.

The interest in explaining the source of the productivity increase is particularly great in light of the traditional literature on French economic history. The agricultural revolution is generally agreed to be a product of the second half of the nineteenth century, with the first half of the century either unchanged from medieval times or changing relatively slowly. Explanations, based on this view of the timing of the agricultural revolution, are obviously inappropriate for explaining the developments in agriculture observed in this study.

An exploratory analysis of the sources of the productivity increase lends considerable support to the hypothesis, suggested by the regional and national patterns, that the decline in fallow and the introduction of mixed farming can account not only for the productivity increase, but for the expansion of cultivated land as well. Mixed farming appears to operate on yield levels not only through the nitrogen added to the soil by including artificial meadows in the rotation, and through the use of manure fertilizer (by stall-feeding expanded fodder crops in winter) but in other ways as well. Some evidence is presented which suggests that mixed farming spread through France both through a process of radial diffusion (farm to farm), and through a diffusion of information from city to city. This study suggests that a more thorough study of the development of mixed farming is essential to a better understanding of the modernization of French agricultural in the nineteenth century.

APPENDIX

Table A: National Components of Rate of Total Increase
(1800-1950)

(rates % of population)

Years	BR	DR	RNI	RNM	RTI
1801-1805	32.2	29.3	2.90	2.20	5.10
1806-1810	31.7	26.3	5.40	7.10	12.50
1811-1815	31.7	26.9	4.80	n.a.	n.a.
1816-1820	32.0	25.3	6.70	-3.60	3.10
1821-1825	31.4	24.7	6.70	-3.80	2.90
1826-1830	30.5	25.5	5.00	n.a.	n.a
1831-1835	29.6	26.0	3.60	3.10	6.70
1836-1840	28.4	23.7	4.70	1.10	5.90
1841-1845	28.1	22.7	5.40	-1.30	4.10
1846-1850	26.7	23.9	2.80	4.00	6.80
1851-1855	26.1	24.1	2.00	0.10	2.10
1856-1860	26.6	23.8	2.80	-1.40	1.40
1861-1865	26.6	22.9	3.70	3.70	7.40
1866-1870	26.0	24.6	1.40	2.20	3.60
1871-1875	25.9	25.1	0.80	-8.00	-8.80
1876-1880	25.7	22.6	3.10	-8.70	-5.60
1881-1885	25.0	22.3	2.70	1.40	4.10
1886-1890	23.3	22.0	1.30	1.60	2.90
1891-1895	22.6	22.4	0.20	0.40	0.60
1896-1900	22.2	20.6	1.60	-0.70	0.90
1901-1905	21.6	19.6	2.00	0.00	2.00
1906-1910	20.2	19.1	1.10	0.60	1.70
1911-1913	18.8	18.4	0.40	1.40	1.80
1921-1925	19.3	17.2	2.10	-3.10	-1.00
1926-1930	18.2	16.8	1.40	6.30	7.70
1931-1935	16.5	15.7	0.80	4.50	5.30
1936-1938	14.8	15.6	-0.80	1.10	0.30
1946-1950	20.9	13.0	7.90	-11.30	-3.40

Source: Toutain, Vol. III, pp. 24, 34-35.

Table B: Regional Components of Rate of Total
Increase: 1801-1910

Region 1: Seine

Years	BR	DR	RNI	RRNM	RTI
1801-1805	35.24	37.32	-2.08	14.46	12.38
1806-1820	32.43	32.00	0.43	12.97	13.41
1821-1825	34.61	30.58	4.03	39.27	43.31
1826-1830	35.83	30.97	4.86	-22.58	-17.72
1831-1835	33.55	33.99	-0.45	34.10	33.65
1836-1840	31.94	27.51	4.43	10.81	15.24
1841-1845	31.47	27.16	4.30	22.25	26.55
1846-1850	30.39	30.46	-0.08	8.34	8.27
1851-1855	29.74	28.09	1.65	37.13	38.78
1856-1860	31.15	25.50	5.66	18.93	24.58
1861-1865	30.13	25.53	4.60	14.62	19.22
1866-1871	28.00	31.06	-3.06	8.33	5.27
1872-1875	28.47	22.61	5.87	14.73	20.60
1876-1880	25.84	24.28	1.56	28.26	29.82
1881-1885	27.13	25.07	2.06	9.17	11.23
1886-1890	25.35	23.53	1.82	17.90	19.72
1891-1895	23.62	22.20	1.42	19.03	20.46
1896-1900	21.96	20.35	1.61	17.19	18.80
1901-1905	20.56	19.18	1.38	8.12	9.51
1906-1910	18.66	18.50	0.16	15.11	15.27

Region 2: Lyon and Marseille

Years	BR	DR	RNI	RRNM	RTI
1801-1805	36.53	33.53	2.99	13.25	16.25
1806-1820	34.35	29.20	5.14	1.95	7.09
1821-1825	36.04	29.88	6.16	4.28	10.44
1826-1830	35.32	30.27	5.06	8.22	13.28
1831-1835	32.65	30.50	2.15	10.16	12.32
1836-1840	32.13	27.98	4.15	3.17	7.32
1841-1845	31.41	26.58	4.82	13.42	18.25
1846-1850	29.67	26.38	3.29	5.71	9.00
1851-1855	28.63	27.08	1.56	16.63	18.19
1856-1860	29.23	25.67	3.56	8.83	12.38
1861-1865	28.23	25.51	2.72	6.78	9.51
1866-1871	26.28	27.54	-1.25	1.00	- 0.19
1872-1875	26.49	24.56	1.93	5.38	7.31
1876-1880	24.93	25.66	-0.73	11.38	10.65

Table B, Region 2 (continued)

Years	BR	DR	RNI	RRNM	RTI
1881-1885	24.23	25.36	-1.13	8.11	6.98
1886-1890	22.78	24.26	-1.68	15.80	14.11
1891-1895	21.75	23.35	-1.60	18.72	17.12
1896-1900	21.10	22.15	-1.05	9.38	8.33
1901-1905	20.20	20.99	-0.79	6.70	5.91
1906-1910	18.52	20.28	-1.76	13.27	11.51

Region 3A: Low % Agriculture and Low Initial Birth Rate

Years	BR	DR	RNI	RRNM	RTI
1801-1805	28.79	26.75	2.04	9.12	11.15
1806-1820	29.23	25.10	4.13	-3.52	0.61
1821-1825	29.71	23.51	6.20	1.25	7.45
1826-1830	27.99	23.99	4.00	0.05	4.06
1831-1835	26.74	25.31	1.43	2.24	3.67
1836-1840	25.61	22.09	3.51	0.44	3.95
1841-1845	25.02	21.89	3.13	0.93	4.06
1846-1850	24.33	23.27	1.06	-0.35	0.70
1851-1855	23.93	23.82	0.11	-0.64	- 0.54
1856-1860	24.75	22.75	2.00	1.93	3.93
1861-1865	24.20	22.65	1.55	0.62	2.16
1866-1871	23.33	25.22	-1.89	0.53	- 1.36
1872-1875	23.92	22.50	1.42	1.89	3.31
1876-1880	23.43	22.62	0.81	1.26	2.07
1881-1885	23.48	22.69	0.79	2.36	3.15
1886-1890	22.90	23.01	-0.11	0.64	0.53
1891-1895	22.31	23.16	-0.85	2.58	1.73
1896-1900	22.30	21.75	0.54	1.21	1.76
1901-1905	21.82	20.39	1.43	1.02	2.45
1906-1910	20.67	19.93	0.74	1.89	2.63

Region 3B: Low % Agriculture and High Initial Birth Rate

Years	BR	DR	RNI	RRNM	RTI
1801-1805	35.79	28.75	7.04	8.53	15.57
1806-1820	33.68	27.23	6.45	-2.86	3.59
1821-1825	33.53	24.62	8.91	2.27	11.18
1826-1830	32.40	25.44	6.96	-0.49	6.47
1831-1835	31.49	26.35	5.14	0.74	5.89
1836-1840	30.76	24.31	6.45	1.02	7.47

Table B, Region 3B (continued)

Years	BR	DR	RNI	RRNM	RTI
1841–1845	29.75	23.81	5.94	0.81	6.75
1846–1850	27.87	24.63	3.24	0.42	3.66
1851–1855	27.66	25.56	2.10	-0.66	1.44
1856–1860	29.17	23.78	5.39	-2.19	3.19
1861–1865	28.79	23.20	5.60	-0.18	5.42
1866–1871	28.11	26.28	1.83	-20.05	-18.22
1872–1875	28.87	22.64	6.22	5.26	11.48
1876–1880	27.80	23.23	4.58	-0.81	3.76
1881–1885	26.82	22.62	4.19	-0.62	3.57
1886–1890	25.10	22.16	2.94	4.47	7.41
1891–1895	24.32	22.42	1.91	7.44	9.35
1896–1900	24.14	20.89	3.25	1.66	4.91
1901–1905	23.06	19.64	3.42	-1.33	2.09
1906–1910	21.11	18.97	2.14	1.95	4.08

Region 4A: Medium % Agriculture and Low Initial Birth Rate

Years	BR	DR	RNI	RRNM	RTI
1801–1805	29.38	29.17	0.21	11.72	11.92
1806–1820	29.04	24.01	5.03	- 3.09	1.94
1821–1825	28.36	22.54	5.82	0.76	6.58
1826–1830	27.52	23.56	3.95	0.58	4.54
1831–1835	26.48	23.41	3.07	0.10	3.17
1836–1840	25.22	21.13	4.09	- 1.33	2.76
1841–1845	25.07	20.39	4.68	- 0.03	4.65
1846–1850	24.15	21.65	2.50	- 1.07	1.43
1851–1855	23.81	21.90	1.91	- 3.45	- 1.54
1856–1860	23.46	22.06	1.40	0.31	1.71
1861–1865	23.43	21.03	2.39	- 1.97	0.42
1866–1871	22.98	25.08	-2.10	- 1.72	- 3.82
1872–1875	23.39	20.98	2.41	0.19	2.60
1876–1880	22.79	21.14	1.65	- 2.32	- 0.67
1881–1885	22.16	20.49	1.68	- 1.34	0.34
1886–1890	21.19	20.85	0.33	- 4.42	- 4.09
1891–1895	19.72	21.12	-1.39	- 3.68	- 5.08
1896–1900	19.84	19.95	-0.11	- 1.48	- 1.59
1901–1905	19.54	19.15	0.39	- 1.90	- 1.51
1906–1910	18.72	19.04	-0.32	- 1.79	- 2.11

Table B (continued)

Region 4B: Medium % Agriculture and High Initial Birth Rate

Years	BR	DR	RNI	RRNM	RTI
1801-1805	35.14	33.26	1.88	7.45	9.33
1806-1820	33.83	27.14	6.69	-2.80	3.89
1821-1825	32.89	26.66	6.22	0.75	6.98
1826-1830	32.01	27.72	4.29	1.00	5.29
1831-1835	31.69	26.82	4.87	1.88	5.29
1836-1840	30.03	25.26	4.77	-1.15	3.62
1841-1845	30.06	22.92	7.14	0.23	7.37
1846-1850	28.50	24.35	4.15	-1.26	2.89
1851-1855	27.53	24.25	3.29	-3.56	-0.27
1856-1860	27.45	25.12	2.33	-1.43	0.90
1861-1865	27.75	22.50	5.25	-1.30	3.95
1866-1871	26.79	26.56	0.23	-2.58	-2.34
1872-1875	27.46	22.33	5.13	-0.67	4.46
1876-1880	26.53	21.58	4.96	-2.55	2.40
1881-1885	25.26	21.19	4.07	-1.33	2.74
1886-1890	23.99	21.47	2.52	-3.16	-0.65
1891-1895	22.25	20.93	1.32	-3.79	-2.47
1896-1900	22.13	19.77	2.36	-2.59	-0.23
1901-1905	21.05	18.84	2.82	-2.91	-0.09
1906-1910	20.20	18.50	1.70	-3.66	-1.96

Region 5A: High % Agriculture and Low Initial Birth Rate

Years	BR	DR	RNI	RRNM	RTI
1801-1805	29.36	24.58	4.78	13.89	18.67
1806-1820	28.04	22.24	5.80	- 7.85	- 2.05
1821-1825	28.64	21.99	6.65	1.16	7.81
1826-1830	28.92	21.50	7.42	- 3.24	4.18
1831-1835	29.02	24.16	4.86	- 0.52	4.34
1836-1840	27.98	22.40	5.58	- 4.29	1.29
1841-1845	28.22	21.49	6.74	- 1.60	5.13
1846-1850	26.43	22.66	3.77	- 4.20	- 0.42
1851-1855	26.20	23.83	2.37	- 5.53	- 3.16
1856-1860	26.15	23.74	2.40	- 3.20	- 0.79
1861-1865	26.85	23.12	3.74	- 4.05	- 0.31
1866-1871	26.63	25.73	0.90	- 3.83	- 2.92
1872-1875	27.02	22.62	4.40	- 2.60	1.80
1876-1880	26.01	22.36	3.64	- 1.84	1.80
1881-1885	24.75	22.31	2.44	- 5.15	- 2.71

Table B, Region 5A (continued)

Years	BR	DR	RNI	RRNM	RTI
1886-1890	23.47	21.99	1.48	-12.37	-10.89
1891-1895	21.32	22.36	-1.04	- 8.17	- 9.21
1896-1900	21.24	21.48	-0.24	- 5.37	- 5.60
1901-1905	20.58	20.34	0.24	- 3.89	- 3.65
1906-1910	19.09	19.85	-0.75	- 5.99	- 6.75

Region 5B: High % Agriculture and High Initial Birth Rate

Years	BR	DR	RNI	RRNM	RTI
1801-1805	34.90	31.42	3.48	7.32	10.80
1806-1820	32.39	26.75	5.64	-2.58	3.06
1821-1825	31.99	25.02	6.97	-0.01	6.96
1826-1830	31.00	25.62	5.38	0.27	5.64
1831-1835	30.61	27.12	3.50	0.27	3.77
1836-1840	29.10	24.57	4.53	-3.62	0.91
1841-1845	29.00	23.45	5.55	-0.82	4.73
1846-1850	27.50	24.23	3.27	-3.27	0.00
1851-1855	27.18	24.11	3.07	-4.85	-1.78
1856-1860	26.96	25.72	1.25	-3.23	-1.98
1861-1865	27.39	23.50	3.89	-2.85	1.04
1866-1871	26.52	26.72	-0.21	-3.88	-4.09
1872-1875	27.21	22.97	4.25	-0.67	3.58
1876-1880	26.27	21.94	4.33	-2.64	1.69
1881-1885	25.46	21.64	3.83	-3.30	0.52
1886-1890	24.32	23.47	0.85	-8.93	-8.08
1891-1895	21.64	21.99	-0.35	-5.75	-6.10
1896-1900	21.93	20.38	1.55	-4.37	-2.82
1901-1905	21.42	19.35	2.07	-3.70	-1.63
1906-1910	20.04	19.22	0.83	-4.64	-3.82

Source: See Table P.

Table C: Inputs and Outputs in French Agriculture
(1750-1950)

Years	Prod[1]	Pop[2]	Prod/Pop	Land[3]	Labor[4]	Prod/ Land	Prod/ Labor
1751-1760	3320	21.5	154.4	21.6	3.5	153.7	948.6
1771-1780	4342	25.6	169.6	23.7	4.1	183.2	1059
1781-1790	4482	27.0	166.0	25.4	4.2	176.5	1067
1803-1812	5140	29.0	177.2	27.0	4.4	190.4	1168
1815-1824	5152	30.50	168.9	28.9	4.6	178.3	1120
1825-1834	5805	32.57	178.2	--	4.8	--	1219
1835-1844	6719	34.23	196.3	27.2	5.0	247.0	1344
1845-1854	7475	35.78	208.9	28.6	5.3	261.4	1410
1855-1864	8586	37.39	229.6	29.4	5.34	292.0	1608
1865-1874	9312	36.10	258.0	--	5.28	--	1764
1875-1884	9267	37.67	246.0	29.1	5.47	318.5	1694
1885-1894	9597	38.34	250.3	28.5	5.04	336.7	1904
1895-1904	10457	38.96	268.4	--	5.52	--	1894
1905-1914	11667	39.60	294.6	26.7	5.33	437.0	2189
1920-1924	11599	39.21	295.8	25.3	4.99	458.5	2324
1925-1934	13579	41.83	324.6	24.3	4.45	558.8	3051
1935-1938	14046	41.91	335.1	23.0	4.22	610.7	3328
1945-1949	11044	40.50	272.7	20.7	4.15	533.5	2661

[1] deflated (millions of 1905-14 francs) final agricultural product,
eed and seed excluded: Toutain, p. 128-129.

Table C (continued)

[2]in millions: Toutain, p. 200.

[3]all crops and artificial meadows and vines (excluding woods and fallow) in millions of hectares : Toutain, pp. 214-215.

[4]male agricultural labor force in millions: Toutain, p. 201.

Table D: Vegetable Production and Its

Components in Value Terms

Crop[1]	1815-1824	1825-1834	1835-1844	1845-1854	1855-1864	1865-1874	1875-1884	1885-1894
Cereals	1837	2087	2409	2741	3051	3100	3153	3270
Potatoes	154	257	386	309	427	498	577	732
Dry Vegetables	94	121	168	212	236	202	166	119
Wine	824	890	855	1059	1070	1336	1018	679
Cider	105	106	117	144	104	134	160	175
Wood	--	--	525	473	486	482	504	508
Forage Crops	--	--	963	1452	1681	2009	2341	2432
Industrial Crops	--	--	326	346	472	508	449	353
Straw	796	887	1001	1117	1207	1255	1305	1168
Fruits, Vegetables, Gardens	--	--	410	459	693	773	705	733
Total	5522[2]	6301[2]	7160	8312	9427	10297	10378	10169
Total[3]	3481	3953	4435	4943	5678	6130	5798	5566

[1] in millions of 1905-14 francs; seeds excluded: Toutain, p. 152.

[2] adjusted for missing observations.

[3] feed excluded: Toutain, p. 128.

Table E: Animal Production and Its

Components in Value Terms

Product	1815-1824	1825-1834	1835-1844	1845-1854	1855-1864	1865-1874	1875-1884	1885-1894
Meat	865	951	1082	1302	1537	1725	1979	2171
Wool	96	106	117	122	110	86	83	94
Silk	16	27	66	65	34	41	27	29
Milk	415	447	558	607	703	703	703	831
Butter and Cheese	296	331	399	435	502	521	521	521
Eggs	122	137	152	167	182	180	190	203
Poultry	123	136	137	166	215	370	462	636
Total	1926	2123	2603	2851	3227	3517	3804	4430
Total[1]	1671	1852	2284	2532	2908	3182	3469	4031

in millions of 1905-14 francs: Toutain, p. 153.

[1]feed excluded: Toutain, p. 128.

Table F: Quantity of Cereal Production

and Its Components

Crop	1815–1824	1825–1834	1835–1844	1845–1854	1855–1864	1865–1874	1875–1884	1885–1894
Wheat	38.79	46.34	52.67	62.25	72.77	74.44	76.57	81.49
Mixed Wheat and Rye	7.71	7.58	8.95	8.54	6.62	5.91	4.52	3.34
Rye	20.6	21.5	22.3	21.0	18.9	18.5	18.47	16.81
Barley	10.15	10.71	11.88	12.37	12.93	12.89	11.47	10.97
Oats	15.51	20.56	25.41	28.81	33.63	33.76	37.41	40.37
Buckwheat	4.03	5.03	5.32	6.8	6.81	7.10	6.50	5.97
Corn and Millet	4.22	4.62	4.85	6.83	6.80	7.45	6.89	7.17
Cereals	104.01	116.34	131.38	146.6	158.46	160.05	161.83	160.1

in millions of quintals, seeds included: Toutain, p. 16.

Table G: National Agricultural Patterns Using
Estimators Developed for Regional Analysis

Years	Prod[1]	Prod/ Pop	Land[2]	Labor[3]	Prod/ Land	Prod/ Labor	Labor/ Land
1815-1819	127.69	4.24	11.32	25.09	11.28	5.09	2.22
1820-1824	151.26	4.92	11.97	26.17	12.63	5.78	2.19
1825-1829	153.46	4.80	12.14	27.26	12.64	5.63	2.24
1830-1834	172.97	5.28	12.56	27.97	13.77	6.18	2.23
1835-1839	183.06	5.44	13.05	28.49	14.03	6.42	2.18
1840-1844	206.70	6.00	13.50	28.73	15.31	7.20	2.13
1845-1849	207.66	5.85	13.79	29.26	15.06	7.10	2.12
1850-1854	210.37	5.87	13.58	29.55	15.50	7.12	2.18
1855-1859	224.00	6.19	13.78	28.09	16.25	7.97	2.04
1860-1864	246.39	6.57	14.27	29.27	17.27	8.42	2.05
1865-1869	234.80	6.33	14.48	29.37	16.21	7.99	2.03
1870-1874	251.19	6.77	14.21	27.75	17.68	9.05	1.95
1875-1879	232.37	6.11	14.36	28.42	16.18	8.18	1.98
1880-1884	263.76	6.71	14.58	--	18.09	--	--
1885-1889	253.95	6.39	14.72	--	17.26	--	--
1890-1894	253.29	6.23	14.96	28.10	16.93	9.04	1.88
1895-1899	260.22	6.48	14.69	--	17.71	--	--

in millions

[1] wheat + rye + barley + oats + 1/5 potatoes

Table G (continued)

[2]wheat + rye + barley + oats + potatoes

[3]total population — population in cities 20,000+ by 1876

Sources:

    production and land: <u>Racoltes des céreales</u>...

    labor: <u>Annuaire Statistique de la France</u>.

Table H: Area under 5 Major Crops, Nationally

Years	Wheat	Rye	Barley	Oats	Potatoes
1815-1819	4.590	2.569	1.122	3.599	.559
1820-1824	4.794	2.764	1.258	3.832	.582
1825-1829	4.925	2.738	1.223	3.873	.607
1830-1834	5.166	2.666	1.283	4.044	.689
1835-1839	5.396	2.638	1.308	4.182	.835
1840-1844	5.603	2.712	1.269	4.207	.978
1845-1849	5.922	2.617	1.218	4.257	.991
1850-1854	6.131	2.361	1.151	4.178	.905
1855-1859	6.555	2.104	1.090	4.170	.955
1860-1864	6.831	2.042	1.115	4.338	1.056
1865-1869	6.972	1.970	1.112	4.414	1.127
1870-1874	6.765	1.896	1.136	4.385	1.162
1875-1879	6.928	1.824	1.037	4.363	1.247
1880-1884	6.910	1.785	1.018	4.558	1.329
1885-1889	6.979	1.632	.923	4.649	1.458
1890-1894	7.018	1.544	.880	4.862	1.538
1895-1899	6.857	1.494	.867	4.826	1.544

in millions of hectares

Source: Racoltes des cereales...

Table I: Yields of 5 Major Crops Nationally

Years	Wheat	Rye	Barley	Oats	Potatoes
1815–1819	9.99	8.48	12.56	14.03	85.17
1820–1824	11.41	10.32	13.60	15.42	76.08
1825–1829	12.09	10.63	12.69	14.08	84.47
1830–1834	12.28	11.82	13.95	16.24	89.24
1835–1839	12.46	11.56	13.86	16.52	97.41
1840–1844	13.58	11.96	15.05	18.22	110.09
1845–1849	13.74	11.83	15.76	18.27	89.07
1850–1854	13.61	11.99	17.18	20.25	76.77
1855–1859	14.18	12.29	17.63	20.60	100.44
1860–1864	14.79	13.32	18.86	22.39	98.74
1865–1869	14.09	13.02	17.29	19.99	100.56
1870–1874	14.94	13.86	18.62	22.58	104.47
1875–1879	13.68	13.44	16.75	20.63	92.41
1880–1884	15.33	14.73	18.46	22.99	100.47
1885–1889	15.33	14.17	18.20	21.88	75.81
1890–1894	15.71	15.84	16.63	19.46	78.16
1895–1899	16.48	15.02	18.35	21.74	80.27

in hectoliters/hectare

Table J: Regional Agricultural Production

Years	3A	3B	4A	4B	5A	5B
1815–1819	41.35	11.11	23.48	26.10	7.45	7.53
1820–1824	47.32	13.46	29.81	30.37	8.56	9.68
1825–1829	44.87	14.90	30.12	32.24	9.50	10.17
1830–1834	50.25	15.30	35.72	36.89	9.89	11.17
1835–1839	53.44	16.02	39.09	38.85	10.32	11.06
1840–1844	60.25	17.52	43.64	45.82	11.42	12.54
1845–1849	62.95	18.99	44.10	43.84	11.47	11.09
1850–1854	65.30	17.82	44.67	44.01	11.63	11.99
1855–1859	67.89	19.76	47.20	48.24	11.64	12.14
1860–1864	74.90	20.82	51.48	51.92	12.64	13.31
1865–1869	70.08	20.00	48.31	49.75	12.54	13.39
1870–1874	76.05	21.92	55.69	56.78	14.11	13.93
1875–1879	69.83	20.80	49.73	53.87	12.93	14.06
1880–1884	79.49	22.57	57.64	62.51	13.82	15.70
1885–1889	75.21	21.16	57.42	59.01	14.28	15.80
1890–1894	72.75	20.19	55.67	61.25	16.35	16.41
1895–1899	76.08	20.28	60.45	63.44	13.87	16.26

in millions of hectoliters

Table K: Regional Hectares Under Cultivation

Years	3A	3B	4A	4B	5A	5B
1815-1819	3.034	.838	2.432	2.567	.891	.783
1820-1824	3.150	.937	2.630	2.737	.912	.818
1825-1829	3.154	.991	2.653	2.770	.945	.839
1830-1834	3.143	1.009	2.827	2.888	.947	.907
1835-1839	3.237	1.033	2.986	3.044	.962	.942
1840-1844	3.292	1.036	3.163	3.184	.994	.964
1845-1849	3.372	1.098	3.194	3.294	.994	.948
1850-1854	3.325	1.085	3.113	3.260	.954	.937
1855-1859	3.360	1.094	3.112	3.343	.965	.971
1860-1864	3.479	1.084	3.192	3.421	.980	.991
1865-1869	3.501	1.091	3.247	3.482	1.004	1.003
1870-1874	3.485	1.109	3.331	3.586	.999	1.005
1875-1879	3.515	1.120	3.326	3.687	1.010	.996
1880-1884	3.533	1.114	3.397	3.769	1.064	1.005
1885-1889	3.551	1.107	3.534	3.717	1.101	1.018
1890-1894	3.544	1.038	3.667	3.920	1.153	.979
1895-1899	3.540	1.012	3.560	3.848	1.129	.965

in millions

Table L: Regional Rural Population

Years	3A	3B	4A	4B	5A	5B
1815-1819	5.483	2.603	5.761	6.254	2.230	2.204
1820-1824	5.689	2.738	5.964	6.497	2.322	2.284
1825-1829	5.895	2.873	6.167	6.740	2.414	2.366
1830-1834	6.015	2.976	6.299	6.906	2.465	2.437
1835-1839	6.107	3.056	6.389	7.109	2.516	2.476
1840-1844	6.203	3.129	6.453	7.189	2.532	2.482
1845-1849	6.293	3.216	6.581	7.427	2.598	2.544
1850-1854	6.302	3.261	6.614	7.528	2.591	2.544
1855-1859	6.197	3.247	5.832	7.256	2.550	2.515
1860-1864	6.284	3.237	6.533	7.467	2.540	2.486
1865-1869	6.313	3.308	6.531	7.570	2.535	2.496
1870-1874	6.195	3.263	6.360	7.451	2.490	2.431
1875-1879	6.248	3.380	6.405	7.561	2.503	2.458
1880-1884	--	--	--	--	--	--
1885-1889	--	--	--	--	--	--
1890-1894	6.251	3.447	6.286	7.191	2.406	2.407
1895-1899	--	--	--	--	--	--

in millions

Table M: Regional Yields

Years	3A	3B	4A	4B	5A	5B
1815-1819	13.63	13.26	9.66	10.16	8.36	9.62
1820-1824	15.02	14.37	11.34	11.10	9.38	11.83
1825-1829	14.23	15.03	11.35	11.64	10.06	12.12
1830-1834	15.99	15.16	12.63	12.78	10.44	12.93
1835-1839	16.51	15.51	13.09	12.76	10.72	11.74
1840-1844	18.30	16.91	13.79	14.39	11.49	13.01
1845-1849	18.67	17.29	13.81	13.31	11.54	11.70
1850-1854	19.64	16.42	14.35	13.50	12.19	12.79
1855-1859	20.21	18.06	15.17	14.43	12.07	12.49
1860-1864	21.53	19.20	16.13	15.18	12.90	13.43
1865-1869	20.02	18.33	14.88	14.29	12.50	13.35
1870-1874	21.82	19.77	16.72	15.84	14.12	13.87
1875-1879	19.87	18.57	14.95	14.61	12.81	14.11
1880-1884	22.50	20.26	16.97	16.58	12.98	15.63
1885-1889	21.18	19.11	16.25	15.88	12.98	15.22
1890-1894	20.53	19.45	15.18	15.63	14.18	16.76
1895-1899	21.49	20.04	16.98	16.48	12.29	16.85

in hectoliters/hectares

Table N: Regional Production/Rural Population

Years	3A	3B	4A	4B	5A	5B
1815-1819	7.54	4.27	4.08	4.17	3.34	3.42
1820-1824	8.32	4.92	5.00	4.67	3.69	4.24
1825-1829	7.61	5.18	4.88	4.78	3.94	4.96
1830-1834	8.35	5.14	5.67	5.34	4.01	4.81
1835-1839	8.75	5.24	6.19	5.46	4.10	4.47
1840-1844	9.71	5.60	6.72	6.37	4.51	5.05
1845-1849	10.00	5.90	6.70	5.90	4.42	4.36
1850-1854	10.36	5.46	6.75	5.85	4.49	4.71
1855-1859	10.95	6.08	8.09	6.65	4.57	4.82
1860-1864	11.92	6.43	7.88	6.95	4.98	5.35
1865-1869	11.10	6.04	7.40	6.57	4.95	5.36
1870-1874	12.28	6.72	8.76	7.62	5.67	5.73
1875-1879	11.18	6.15	7.76	7.12	5.17	5.72
1880-1884	--	--	--	--	--	--
1885-1889	--	--	--	--	--	--
1890-1894	11.64	5.86	8.86	8.52	6.79	6.82
1895-1899	--	--	--	--	--	--

in hectoliters/population

Table O: Regional Rural Population/Hectares

Years	3A	3B	4A	4B	5A	5B
1815–1819	1.81	3.11	2.37	2.44	2.50	2.82
1820–1824	1.81	2.92	2.27	2.37	2.54	2.79
1825–1829	1.87	2.90	2.32	2.43	2.56	2.82
1830–1834	1.91	2.95	2.23	2.39	2.60	2.69
1835–1839	1.89	2.96	2.14	2.34	2.62	2.63
1840–1844	1.88	3.02	2.04	2.26	2.55	2.57
1845–1849	1.87	2.93	2.06	2.25	2.61	2.68
1850–1854	1.90	3.01	2.12	2.31	2.72	2.72
1855–1859	1.84	2.97	1.87	2.17	2.64	2.59
1860–1864	1.81	2.99	2.05	2.18	2.59	2.51
1865–1869	1.80	3.03	2.01	2.17	2.53	2.49
1870–1874	1.78	2.94	1.91	2.08	2.49	2.42
1875–1879	1.78	3.02	1.93	2.05	2.48	2.47
1880–1884	--	--	--	--	--	--
1885–1889	--	--	--	--	--	--
1890–1894	1.76	3.32	1.71	1.83	2.09	2.46
1895–1899	--	--	--	--	--	--

in population/hectares

Table P: Departmental Demographic Variables

Period 1 (1815-24 to 1840-49):

Department	BR	DR	RNI	RRNM	RTI	RNI_0	GRP
Ain	29.86	25.81	4.05	0.14	4.19	2.79	11.71
Aisne	29.01	23.48	5.53	0.98	6.52	6.67	18.84
Allier	31.43	27.17	4.26	1.88	6.15	4.31	16.70
Alpes-B.	30.83	28.28	2.55	-1.93	0.61	5.96	4.93
Alpes-H.	32.16	27.78	4.38	-1.58	2.80	5.54	9.62
Ardèche	32.76	24.19	8.57	-0.60	7.97	8.84	24.73
Ardenne	28.13	20.78	7.35	-0.15	7.19	7.93	22.41
Ariege	29.57	21.99	7.57	-3.25	4.33	8.28	15.18
Aube	25.54	22.23	3.31	1.34	4.66	3.52	14.54
Aude	29.30	24.09	5.21	-0.71	4.50	7.01	28.56
Aveyron	29.79	22.82	6.96	-1.97	4.99	5.56	14.64
Calvados	20.86	20.78	0.08	-0.17	-0.10	1.97	- 0.23
Cantal	26.34	21.30	5.04	-4.88	0.16	4.62	3.32
Charente	24.81	21.67	3.14	0.08	3.23	4.31	7.94
Charente-I.	25.87	23.85	2.02	2.57	4.60	1.29	13.49
Cher	34.59	28.29	6.30	1.88	8.18	7.38	22.24
Corrèze	33.00	26.65	6.33	-1.00	5.33	7.36	16.14
Côte-d'Or	26.53	22.49	4.03	-0.32	3.71	2.63	9.09
Côtes-du-N.	32.02	25.62	6.40	-1.88	4.52	6.75	13.77
Creuse	28.15	21.19	6.96	-2.19	4.77	7.27	14.83
Dordogne	28.42	24.71	3.70	-0.03	3.66	4.23	10.36
Doubs	28.68	22.37	6.31	0.38	6.70	6.27	16.70
Drôme	29.75	24.52	5.22	0.70	5.94	7.17	16.10
Eure	21.49	22.24	-0.75	0.84	-0.03	1.87	1.69
Eure-et-L.	25.89	23.18	3.35	0.27	3.64	3.21	9.60
Finistère	35.47	29.37	6.10	2.08	8.19	4.23	20.65
Gard	33.06	26.29	6.76	-0.10	6.66	6.97	15.37
Garonne-H.	27.39	22.22	5.19	1.74	6.84	6.04	14.43
Gers	22.58	21.58	1.00	-0.33	0.67	3.87	4.49
Gironde	25.64	22.90	2.74	2.68	5.43	2.48	10.18
Hérault	30.65	26.40	4.25	1.84	6.10	6.10	14.72
Ille-et-V.	30.04	27.03	3.01	-0.51	2.49	1.80	3.99
Indre	31.26	25.15	6.10	-0.56	5.54	5.67	14.63
Indre-et-L.	24.69	21.88	2.81	0.90	3.71	3.09	8.13
Isère	30.43	23.63	6.79	-0.89	5.90	8.57	17.87
Jura	27.48	24.35	3.13	-1.88	1.25	5.53	4.76
Landes	31.42	26.11	5.30	0.18	5.49	3.71	16.35
Loir-et-C.	30.25	25.88	4.37	0.31	3.54	2.72	11.56

Table P, Period 1 (continued)

Department	BR*	DR*	RNI*	RRNM*	RTI*	RNI₀*	GRP**
Loire	34.96	26.35	8.60	2.03	10.64	8.51	23.80
Loire-H.	29.93	23.26	6.65	-3.47	3.19	5.34	10.95
Loire-I.	28.56	23.75	4.81	1.68	6.99	5.76	15.78
Loiret	31.24	26.43	4.31	0.43	5.26	1.91	13.85
Lot	26.27	22.49	3.78	-1.33	2.44	4.34	6.99
Lot-et-G.	21.81	21.69	0.12	1.14	1.17	3.48	4.87
Lozère	29.69	23.93	5.77	-3.19	2.58	6.21	7.01
Maine-et-L.	24.78	22.10	2.68	2.37	5.06	5.39	11.99
Manche	22.94	20.86	2.08	-1.65	0.37	3.86	- 0.25
Marne	28.42	24.86	3.55	2.88	6.45	3.39	16.07
Marne-H.	25.70	20.85	4.84	-0.17	4.68	5.17	12.35
Mayenne	26.93	22.15	4.77	-1.92	2.85	3.53	6.70
Meuse	27.59	22.45	5.14	-1.13	4.01	5.92	11.77
Morbihan	32.06	27.15	4.91	-0.29	4.62	3.76	11.83
Nièvre	33.09	26.88	6.20	1.21	7.92	5.49	25.22
Nord	33.01	26.84	6.17	2.01	8.20	6.81	22.70
Oise	25.54	23.11	2.43	-0.03	2.40	2.89	8.03
Orne	21.08	18.45	2.61	-1.30	1.31	3.05	4.54
Pas-de-C.	29.10	23.99	5.10	-1.74	3.36	6.17	7.25
Puy-de-D.	27.57	22.98	4.59	-2.07	2.52	5.07	8.42
Pyrénées-B.	25.87	20.91	4.96	-1.22	3.41	6.53	13.00
Pyrénées-H.	26.13	19.32	6.80	-1.19	5.61	8.61	16.62
Pyrénées-O.	36.84	29.12	7.72	0.29	8.02	6.76	21.09
Saône-H.	29.20	21.86	7.33	-3.33	4.00	6.45	12.63
Saône-et-L.	31.44	25.88	5.56	-0.84	4.77	5.48	12.10
Sarthe	25.09	20.43	4.65	-1.35	3.30	5.22	9.07
Seine-I.	29.25	25.73	3.52	1.48	5.00	4.59	13.87
Seine-et-M.	28.28	25.07	3.20	1.11	4.32	3.74	12.22
Seine-et-O.	25.77	25.01	0.76	2.81	3.57	1.67	10.82
Sèvres-D.	25.94	20.53	5.40	-0.56	4.84	5.75	14.27
Somme	26.93	23.40	3.53	0.29	3.83	5.65	16.62
Tarn	29.25	23.39	5.86	-0.99	4.87	7.03	13.68
Tarn-et-G.	23.81	22.43	1.37	-1.45	-0.08	3.01	2.21
Var	27.85	27.96	-0.11	5.44	5.32	2.98	4.60
Vaucluse	33.24	28.55	4.68	0.78	5.49	6.28	14.84
Vendee	29.43	23.67	5.75	0.65	6.41	5.99	18.82
Vienne	27.50	21.07	6.43	0.11	6.55	5.90	17.55
Vienne-H.	34.20	29.43	4.77	0.75	5.31	4.90	11.83
Vosges	28.95	21.63	7.31	-1.38	5.93	9.11	19.61
Yonne	26.81	22.68	4.17	0.38	4.51	2.99	12.60

Table P, Period 1 (continued)

Figures actually for 1821-25 to 1846-50

  *   average rates o/oo of population

  ** % change during the period

GRP = growth in rural population.

Table P: Departmental Demographic Variables

Period 2 (1840-49 to 1865-74):

Department	BR	DR	RNI	RRNM	RTI	RNI$_1$	GRP	TMFR	% LIT
Ain	24.41	23.81	1.04	-0.59	0.01	4.05	- 1.11	1.58	89.6
Aisne	24.64	23.38	1.81	-0.83	0.42	5.53	- 2.99	1.48	85.1
Allier	28.15	21.72	6.34	0.60	7.04	4.26	13.28	1.90	66.7
Alpes-B.	26.62	27.66	-0.69	-3.68	-4.72	2.55	-11.07	1.88	83.7
Alpes-H.	29.29	29.51	1.16	-3.32	-3.54	4.38	-10.67	2.35	90.3
Ardèche	30.81	26.06	5.57	-3.86	0.60	8.57	0.17	2.48	78.2
Ardenne	23.54	20.72	3.35	-1.46	0.28	7.35	- 2.02	1.58	95.2
Ariege	26.74	24.03	3.36	-6.00	-3.29	7.57	- 8.96	2.05	70.9
Aube	20.78	21.51	-0.12	-0.01	-0.74	3.31	- 7.61	1.06	95.6
Aude	25.82	23.81	2.68	-0.37	1.63	5.21	- 2.61	1.67	79.3
Aveyron	29.81	24.77	5.17	-2.79	2.25	6.96	3.43	2.54	87.9
Calvados	19.82	23.20	-2.85	0.20	-3.21	0.08	- 9.13	1.41	90.8
Cantal	25.29	22.78	2.79	-6.38	-3.87	5.04	-10.98	2.20	81.8
Charente	22.69	22.65	3.70	-0.18	-1.40	3.14	- 4.83	1.33	86.0
Charente-I.	22.39	22.15	0.52	-0.27	-0.01	2.02	- 2.02	1.37	86.0
Cher	30.01	22.70	7.88	-1.71	5.60	6.30	12.73	1.92	71.1
Corrèze	30.70	27.41	3.68	-3.86	0.26	6.33	- 4.67	2.25	56.1
Côte-d'Or	21.80	22.19	0.29	-1.05	-0.25	4.03	- 9.40	1.46	94.6
Côtes-du-N.	30.20	25.56	4.76	-4.23	0.41	6.40	- 0.99	2.77	58.7
Creuse	24.25	19.90	5.24	-5.10	-0.76	6.96	- 3.86	1.65	81.7
Dordogne	26.62	24.32	2.16	-2.79	-0.50	3.70	- 6.62	1.71	69.4
Doubs	26.08	23.47	2.65	-0.54	2.07	6.31	- 4.18	2.11	98.4
Drôme	25.88	24.56	2.03	-1.04	0.28	5.22	- 2.10	1.76	86.1
Eure	19.40	23.27	-2.39	-0.13	-4.01	-0.75	-10.72	1.23	83.6
Eure-et-L.	23.87	24.14	0.19	-0.62	-0.90	3.35	- 4.34	1.47	89.9

Table P, Period 2 (continued)

Department	BR	DR	RNI	RRNM	RTI	RNI1	GRP	TMFR	% LIT
Finistère	33.81	28.52	5.19	-1.95	3.28	6.10	4.98	2.90	66.6
Gard	30.61	28.24	3.04	-0.27	2.10	6.76	2.90	1.91	71.9
Garonne-H.	22.43	21.34	1.41	-1.25	-0.16	5.19	-8.56	1.41	76.7
Gers	19.49	21.34	-1.26	-1.47	-3.32	1.00	-9.58	1.28	78.4
Gironde	22.38	21.21	1.39	5.79	6.96	2.74	7.16	1.28	82.5
Hérault	27.04	26.39	1.26	4.35	5.00	4.25	4.40	1.90	81.2
Ille-et-V.	27.96	24.78	3.23	-0.69	2.49	3.01	2.62	2.34	70.4
Indre	27.78	21.72	6.50	-3.81	2.22	6.10	5.20	1.78	61.7
Indre-et-L.	21.22	20.62	1.06	1.05	1.65	2.81	-16.80	1.28	84.1
Isère	25.96	25.07	1.66	-1.75	-0.85	6.79	-8.12	1.87	85.5
Jura	24.11	24.79	-0.66	-2.09	-2.77	3.13	-9.02	1.94	91.4
Lande	28.42	22.54	5.48	-5.09	0.78	5.30	0.77	1.96	69.9
Loir-et-C.	26.01	22.76	3.53	-0.99	2.25	4.37	4.06	1.64	80.0
Loire	31.32	24.29	7.22	2.20	9.23	8.60	7.30	2.32	75.8
Loire-H.	28.55	23.95	4.79	-3.70	0.91	6.65	0.51	2.44	69.5
Loire-I.	26.32	20.88	5.73	0.33	5.77	4.81	14.66	2.21	79.4
Loiret	27.92	24.25	4.15	-0.60	3.07	4.31	7.42	1.75	84.4
Lot	23.49	22.46	1.62	-3.12	-2.11	3.78	-4.47	1.59	76.9
Lot-et-G.	18.79	21.95	-2.95	0.29	-2.86	0.12	-7.77	1.06	83.0
Lozère	30.56	25.24	5.22	-6.23	-9.10	5.77	-5.68	2.72	78.2
Maine-et-L.	21.99	21.26	1.16	0.20	0.93	2.68	-0.04	1.48	79.4
Manche	21.79	22.42	-0.28	-2.89	-3.52	2.08	-11.76	1.82	91.2
Marne	24.90	23.54	1.81	2.64	4.00	3.55	3.19	1.47	92.5
Marne-H.	22.27	21.90	0.65	-1.40	-1.04	4.84	-4.15	1.52	97.8
Mayenne	24.39	22.70	2.13	-2.90	-1.23	4.77	-7.50	1.96	70.2
Meuse	22.52	22.13	0.67	-3.20	-2.82	5.14	-12.58	1.43	97.4
Morbihan	30.20	26.08	4.30	-1.26	2.70	4.91	2.10	2.57	53.7

Table P, Period 2 (continued)

Department	BR	DR	RNI*	RRNM	RTI	RNI1	GRP	TMFR	% LIT
Nièvre	28.06	23.02	5.53	-2.37	2.66	6.20	3.96	1.76	69.7
Nord	32.43	24.45	7.26	1.98	9.97	6.17	16.02	2.65	77.7
Oise	23.04	24.04	-0.38	0.80	-0.20	2.43	-2.27	1.36	88.5
Orne	18.98	20.93	-1.10	-1.73	-3.86	2.61	-9.92	1.38	87.8
Pas-de-C.	28.96	23.28	5.10	-1.05	4.62	5.10	7.75	2.33	77.7
Puy-de-D.	23.84	23.16	1.34	-2.36	-0.12	4.59	-6.77	1.67	79.3
Pyrénées-B.	25.16	22.82	2.45	-4.10	-1.76	4.96	-12.12	2.27	77.3
Pyrénées-H.	22.90	21.03	2.54	-3.45	-1.58	6.80	-8.14	1.91	93.5
Pyrénées-O.	32.74	27.60	5.36	-1.92	3.21	7.72	4.04	2.32	83.1
Saône-H.	24.81	23.11	2.17	-5.82	-4.12	7.33	-12.68	1.79	95.2
Saône-et-L.	28.24	23.19	4.99	-2.02	3.02	5.56	2.27	1.83	88.7
Sarthe	21.33	21.87	0.14	-1.33	-1.87	4.65	-10.82	1.37	77.0
Seine-I.	29.10	27.14	2.15	-0.11	1.84	3.52	6.14	2.23	77.6
Seine-et-M.	24.43	23.65	1.14	0.26	1.04	3.20	0.38	1.49	93.5
Seine-et-O.	23.02	23.94	-0.62	5.80	4.88	0.76	17.82	1.49	94.2
Sèvres-D.	24.46	20.84	3.87	0.57	4.19	5.40	2.59	1.75	77.6
Somme	24.21	23.58	0.99	-1.31	0.22	3.53	5.70	1.56	83.4
Tarn	25.60	22.87	3.05	-2.66	0.06	5.86	3.17	1.78	72.5
Tarn-et-G.	20.71	22.53	-1.34	-1.04	-2.87	1.37	9.85	1.63	75.1
Var	24.11	26.50	-2.24	-2.86	-5.26	-0.11	-21.71	1.63	85.1
Vaucluse	28.01	25.77	2.84	-2.88	-0.64	4.68	0.57	1.87	82.2
Vendee	27.25	22.22	5.66	-1.67	3.27	5.75	6.72	1.89	73.8
Vienne	25.09	21.35	4.28	-1.05	2.68	6.43	3.17	1.68	80.0
Vienne-H.	30.81	26.67	4.46	-1.54	2.59	4.77	2.64	1.90	58.7
Vosges	25.85	23.09	3.03	-3.77	-1.01	7.31	8.16	1.76	98.3
Yonne	22.40	21.92	1.44	-1.88	-1.40	4.12	3.00	1.31	94.0

Table P, Period 2 (continued)

* figures actually for 1846-50 to 1872-75 except RNI_2 (1841-45 to 1866-71)

Sources:

population – Annuaire Statistique de la France, 1961.

births, deaths, city population – Territoire et Population, 1837.

Annuaire Statistique de la France, 1878.

Total Marital Fertility Rate and % Literacy of Conscriptees – Encyclopédie Dictionnaire des Sciences Médicales.

191

Table Q: Departmental Agricultural Variables

Period 1 (1815-24 to 1840-49):

Department	GPR	GY	GH	RGH	IY	LP	RP/U
Ain	40.85	52	2.84	6.58	9.68	38.05	95.54
Aisne	31.06	23	8.16	6.85	18.77	48.50	83.67
Allier	55.77	41	21.68	22.56	10.81	70.82	44.62
Alpes-B.	11.24	6	27.50	20.90	8.90	72.70	49.60
Alpes-H.	10.90	18	9.81	8.71	14.19	77.83	45.96
Ardèche	79.13	62	5.83	4.11	7.94	60.34	102.85
Ardenne	28.87	38	- 2.16	- 0.91	12.55	45.12	79.96
Ariege	98.30	39	33.94	38.88	9.24	61.21	96.66
Aube	41.42	26	19.36	18.44	9.70	31.22	56.43
Aude	-12.54	3	- 1.57	- 3.51	11.87	49.74	52.82
Aveyron	58.05	47	28.86	28.87	9.51	74.42	58.99
Calvados	13.22	3	10.88	5.94	15.18	57.05	99.23
Cantal	-10.99	5	- 4.49	- 6.14	9.12	72.32	61.46
Charente	103.40	76	28.84	15.93	6.76	43.18	77.57
Charente-I.	40.13	41	7.68	9.86	7.02	38.97	77.23
Cher	54.35	19	8.34	4.50	8.79	58.72	43.59
Corrèze	2.67	- 6	44.72	39.29	8.41	60.50	99.61
Côte-d'Or	54.73	54	16.50	16.13	9.83	29.50	76.07
Côtes-du-N.	30.19	19	43.18	33.05	17.48	63.75	104.96
Creuse	57.54	43	29.53	29.46	8.00	58.40	68.88
Dordogne	33.97	18	12.07	13.34	4.32	32.85	99.86
Doubs	83.60	33	32.60	23.84	13.58	71.50	69.54
Drôme	35.48	6	33.62	36.62	10.40	52.03	91.41
Eure	30.33	59	-10.40	-14.15	13.43	44.64	100.36
Eure-et-L.	28.94	27	18.59	16.34	13.48	48.32	51.41
Finistère	41.50	7	40.16	36.17	21.98	69.56	90.87
Gard	31.11	51	-10.50	-13.39	11.36	57.95	92.96
Garonne-H.	3.47	10	5.83	- 1.34	11.21	43.95	68.82
Gers	35.32	22	14.73	13.37	7.40	44.25	60.50
Gironde	46.61	27	13.18	11.24	6.94	41.93	109.36
Hérault	19.79	23	21.09	19.38	12.42	52.23	75.86
Ille-et-V.	47.75	52	4.72	2.67	12.47	52.32	93.09
Indre	11.94	42	3.56	4.88	8.50	63.25	45.74
Indre-et-L.	62.72	36	41.26	30.95	8.97	59.56	60.72
Isère	93.83	57	42.05	33.67	13.03	52.04	119.63
Jura	59.36	33	25.71	23.86	11.20	57.90	112.22
Landes	57.59	19	70.93	61.10	7.20	34.70	126.26
Loir-et-C.	17.49	3	33.31	30.34	10.04	55.08	55.55

Table Q, Period 1 (continued)

Department	GPR	GY	GH	RGH	IY	LP	RP/U
Loire	73.01	30	38.74	40.26	8.94	48.80	106.64
Loire-H.	25.05	21	6.97	16.06	10.66	55.58	97.61
Loire-I.	159.84	12	126.39	102.99	12.54	74.96	66.40
Loiret	69.12	43	12.18	9.63	10.54	47.19	56.08
Lot	12.20	16	1.89	6.81	6.77	17.35	101.92
Lot-et-G.	11.96	29	7.62	9.29	7.78	27.26	89.76
Lozère	9.01	46	5.61	11.55	9.77	80.29	43.11
Maine-et-L.	55.33	16	61.94	57.99	13.08	65.91	71.00
Manche	20.85	5	17.70	8.26	16.39	53.56	111.38
Marne	23.10	35	- 7.19	- 8.17	10.56	15.10	48.66
Marne-H.	105.97	75	16.65	17.76	7.68	32.25	71.99
Mayenne	92.26	68	22.45	15.24	10.05	59.23	72.50
Meuse	41.51	31	8.48	8.55	10.85	35.74	79.92
Morbihan	24.00	87	-16.40	-12.35	8.71	42.49	82.34
Nièvre	92.00	49	29.05	26.90	9.14	69.50	58.68
Nord	19.33	14	16.62	14.37	24.10	56.16	167.00
Oise	31.48	18	6.84	7.63	18.34	50.48	89.89
Orne	6.43	34	5.85	9.95	11.35	52.53	88.05
Pas-de-C.	29.97	21	4.30	5.43	21.96	58.04	103.38
Puy-de-D.	6.95	13	7.86	5.21	12.24	46.36	102.51
Pyrénées-B.	13.74	12	18.66	21.53	10.27	55.37	116.18
Pyrénées-H.	12.07	19	- 3.45	1.45	13.28	54.89	93.26
Pyrénées-O.	28.47	29	7.28	5.25	9.33	51.16	79.36
Saône-H.	26.85	16	31.07	27.65	13.20	43.29	114.86
Saône-et-L.	52.00	17	24.17	21.71	9.85	62.83	84.63
Sarthe	29.10	4	24.51	22.69	11.76	58.93	84.42
Seine-I.	37.70	42	14.11	14.70	16.86	72.18	115.11
Seine-et-M.	44.29	31	2.31	0.09	15.18	36.74	79.05
Seine-et-O.	0.76	8	7.15	5.84	21.00	29.77	120.65
Sèvres-D.	62.58	23	38.24	35.21	11.85	62.97	51.28
Somme	39.50	19	64.30	26.95	18.95	50.83	86.92
Tarn	11.07	5	7.27	4.86	9.35	41.48	76.26
Tarn-et-G.	22.94	28	4.52	- 6.76	8.33	30.41	78.16
Var	38.06	55	19.08	12.46	6.56	14.05	161.26
Vaucluse	91.97	22	40.92	24.10	9.99	45.92	134.87
Vendee	115.40	36	76.50	91.74	9.85	72.14	53.67
Vienne	77.49	25	43.65	43.21	9.88	61.05	45.48
Vienne-H.	- 9.95	22	- 1.60	- 7.27	10.01	50.54	67.95
Vosges	66.79	12	35.90	41.25	16.29	54.55	127.76
Yonne	117.90	77	19.50	20.65	7.44	**28.54**	86.85

Table Q, Period 1 (continued)

1. Growth in Production, Growth in Yields, Growth in Hectares (5 crops), Revised Growth in Hectares (8 crops) all in % change over the period.

2. Initial Yields in Hectoliters/Hectare.

3. Land Potential is % of cultivatable land unused.

4. Rural Population/Hectares is a density measure.

5. % Agriculture same as given for Period 2 (actually for 1891).

Table Q: Departmental Agricultural Variables

Period 2 (1840-49 to 1865-74):

Department	GPR	GY	GH	%Ag	IY	LP	RP/U
Ain	20.53	14	- 1	62	14.70	33.47	106.73
Aisne	10.97	5	11	38	23.16	46.92	99.43
Allier	34.94	14	0	54	15.25	64.00	52.07
Alpes-B.	2.33	0	0	73	9.40	65.04	52.05
Alpes-H.	11.46	5	3	72	16.70	79.60	50.38
Ardèche	36.48	24	8	70	12.84	60.08	128.29
Ardenne	29.27	18	5	29	17.33	36.08	97.88
Ariege	- 0.11	9	4.75	68	12.86	51.00	111.33
Aube	30.80	26	2.50	41	12.24	25.72	64.65
Aude	0.84	14	- 7.24	68	12.26	57.82	67.91
Aveyron	14.44	- 1	3.85	68	13.98	66.78	67.63
Calvados	- 1.16	5	-11.27	48	15.71	52.68	99.00
Cantal	27.71	34	-20.51	74	9.58	71.81	63.50
Charente	1.24	- 5	3.17	61	11.90	33.70	83.73
Charente-I.	57.18	31	9.80	56	9.92	37.04	87.66
Cher	36.28	32	5.45	53	10.42	55.80	53.29
Corrèze	63.19	46	17.78	64	7.88	42.94	115.31
Côte-d'Or	23.13	16	3.02	46	15.14	18.29	82.99
Côtes-du-N.	21.88	-24	23.72	71	20.72	56.12	119.42
Creuse	- 8.09	9	-28.16	63	11.41	46.92	79.09
Dordogne	136.20	83	20.19	66	5.11	26.25	110.21
Doubs	33.26	6	9.75	45	18.06	64.67	81.16
Drôme	31.07	- 8	21.73	64	11 07	41.54	106.13
Eure	32.18	- 1	22.19	45	21.40	57.17	102.06
Eure-et-L.	65.44	32	11.78	51	17.16	40.56	56.35
Finistère	-13.67	-17	0	58	23.58	52.57	109.63
Gard	27.97	-13	43.12	48	17.16	63.02	107.25
Garonne-H.	17.99	20	0.79	52	12.38	40.09	78.75
Gers	34.17	43	- 9.35	72	9.02	37.41	63.22
Gironde	94.86	71	10.51	41	8.82	39.50	120.50
Hérault	-17.02	-10	-13.13	47	15.32	42.71	87.04
Ille-et-V.	24.56	-16	31.67	61	18.92	50.42	96.81
Indre	64.36	19	5.19	61	12.06	60.74	52.44
Indre-et-L.	20.74	3	- 5.22	50	12.24	38.98	65.66
Isère	40.97	-23	21.25	53	20.48	55.95	141.01
Jura	1.18	1	4.16	58	14.94	50.91	117.57
Lande	9.84	14	-23.93	66	8.60	- 3.19	146.91

Table Q, Period 2 (continued)

Department	GPR	GY	GH	%Ag	IY	LP	RP/U
Loir-et-C.	62.78	50	5.79	62	10.34	43.77	61.98
Loire	- 4.43	4	7.67	32	11.58	40.17	132.03
Loire-H	37.87	15	9.99	68	12.90	48.75	108.31
Loire-I.	11.57	12	0.69	53	14.09	50.04	76.88
Loiret	62.13	37	16.52	50	15.03	42.85	63.85
Lot	68.40	12	0	77	7.86	6.88	109.06
Lot-et-G.	43.14	45	-22.35	62	10.02	18.52	94.13
Lozère	75.20	- 1	34.46	72	13.96	79.83	46.13
Maine-et-L.	39.79	8	6.73	53	15.22	52.35	79.52
Manche	- 4.16	- 5	- 1.26	56	17.18	49.48	111.11
Marne	- 6.13	14	-18.16	38	14.26	21.17	56.48
Marne-H.	12.56	26	- 3.35	41	13.42	20.45	80.89
Mayenne	31.74	10	8.66	57	16.86	52.01	77.36
Meuse	22.30	15	3.35	39	14.26	33.37	89.33
Morbihan	26.38	1	0.60	62	16.27	52.17	92.09
Nièvre	44.49	10	22.19	55	13.64	60.73	73.48
Nord	28.22	9	11.87	23	27.54	50.47	204.91
Oise	47.66	16	28.48	36	21.58	50.62	97.11
Orne	14.36	10	- 2.26	52	15.24	52.94	92.05
Pas-de-C.	25.46	0	39.01	35	26.48	53.29	110.88
Puy-de-D.	21.93	27	- 1.66	68	13.87	43.30	111.15
Pyrénées-B.	40.66	4	3.68	56	11.54	49.84	131.29
Pyrénées-H.	-29.92	-12	-20.17	65	15.84	51.54	108.76
Pyrénées-O.	46.35	35	- 1.70	56	12.03	48.99	96.10
Saône-H.	16.71	9	6.68	56	15.28	35.86	129.37
Saône-et-L.	73.03	33	11.41	55	11.52	56.66	94.28
Sarthe	21.96	19	4.38	55	12.22	47.03	92.07
Seine-I.	- 2.59	-10	0.12	25	23.90	45.96	131.08
Seine-et-M.	36.08	24	3.77	43	19.88	29.50	88.71
Seine-et-O.	29.58	19	1.30	33	22.65	24.45	133.71
Sèvres-D.	17.53	11	6.22	64	14.59	54.74	58.60
Somme	9.04	1	10.21	36	22.62	40.86	101.37
Tarn	51.69	35	3.06	54	9.78	37.69	86.70
Tarn-et-G.	53.60	25	4.09	62	10.66	33.33	79.90
Var	32.02	30	-27.87	40	10.17	- 0.87	168.68
Vaucluse	87.18	16	40.18	52	12.14	31.81	154.90
Vendée	- 5.90	- 8	-19.68	63	13.35	51.87	63.77
Vienne	35.26	21	0.85	59	12.36	48.77	53.46
Vienne-H.	55.06	14	3.67	56	12.18	61.50	75.99
Vosges	- 6.25	12	6.75	40	18.25	28.55	152.82
Yonne	6.57	9	8.34	57	13.18	17.16	97.80

Table R: Mixed Farming Variables for Departments (1852)

Departments	Yield	% Fallow	% Art. M.	Manure/H
Ain	15.43	11.08	9.67	187
Aisne	24.34	17.93	8.93	368
Allier	16.10	75.83	14.90	122
Alpes-B.	11.82	60.50	14.47	143
Alpes-H.	18.24	65.03	20.02	111
Ardèche	14.69	36.25	5.15	217
Ardenne	16.64	25.25	28.28	302
Ariege	13.01	23.80	11.73	153
Aube	12.99	29.07	18.91	215
Aude	13.88	38.89	22.78	160
Aveyron	12.11	67.95	10.90	156
Bouche-de-R.	12.87	35.71	10.49	242
Calvados	18.80	14.60	24.42	256
Cantal	10.62	62.45	1.75	130
Charente	10.30	12.13	9.38	135
Charente-I.	12.93	25.53	8.86	149
Cher	11.41	43.11	36.94	156
Corrèze	7.52	27.35	1.07	144
Côte-d'Or	15.15	22.35	14.63	124
Côte-du-N.	19.09	45.33	9.58	101
Creuse	10.35	47.96	0.59	108
Dordogne	7.17	14.69	5.04	161
Doubs	17.69	11.71	26.91	159
Drôme	10.17	27.80	21.83	282
Eure	19.20	19.53	28.78	177
Eure-et-L.	18.10	19.37	35.09	209
Finistère	26.74	23.54	7.46	101
Gard	13.98	41.94	29.03	240
Garonne-H.	13.42	35.66	15.56	137
Gers	11.91	37.64	11.23	151
Gironde	11.35	25.11	8.09	147
Hérault	11.89	53.78	23.81	232
Ille-et-V.	16.65	22.68	9.64	209
Indre	13.08	54.73	12.94	169
Indre-et-L.	10.42	33.71	12.07	138
Isère	14.97	15.95	15.12	215
Jura	15.18	19.41	26.96	166
Lande	10.11	8.97	1.72	191
Loir-et-C.	11.13	31.37	15.70	150

Table R (continued)

Department	Yield	% Fallow	% Art. M.	Manure/H
Loire	10.21	46.09	6.25	153
Loire-H.	12.94	45.68	2.45	106
Loire-I.	15.49	42.32	8.36	159
Loiret	16.03	39.46	29.47	207
Lot	8.64	20.59	3.03	136
Lot-et-G.	10.93	30.26	10.24	141
Lozère	13.05	91.06	3.46	130
Maine-et-L.	14.57	34.11	18.86	172
Manche	18.34	10.09	23.70	230
Marne	20.25	38.16	21.32	309
Marne-H.	12.84	27.90	9.36	155
Mayenne	17.47	37.52	28.09	122
Meurthe	16.46	23.94	14.45	101
Meuse	15.02	26.13	11.69	181
Morbihan	14.25	14.35	0.52	130
Moselle	16.22	19.53	17.23	98
Nièvre	14.15	56.40	23.27	129
Nord	27.37	7.51	22.28	272
Oise	23.41	20.86	35.74	323
Orne	13.68	28.29	23.89	196
Pas-de-C.	27.71	17.48	22.31	292
Puy-de-D.	12.86	48.01	7.19	164
Pyrénées-B.	13.69	7.52	2.39	204
Pyrénées-H.	16.83	21.17	3.97	143
Pyrénées-O.	15.17	53.90	15.93	174
Rhin-B.	20.60	5.27	13.94	98
Rhin-H.	17.27	15.28	15.10	81
Rhone	17.21	39.92	17.22	118
Saône-H.	14.34	24.53	11.25	113
Saône-et-L.	11.29	50.07	7.78	106
Sarthe	14.09	31.55	26.65	151
Seine	28.63	0.86	18.07	173
Seine-I.	21.99	10.64	28.51	309
Seine-et-M.	19.35	28.51	32.58	297
Seine-et-O.	22.77	16.27	27.41	281
Sèvres-D.	15.85	69.82	20.23	173
Somme	24.95	20.05	20.95	317
Tarn	10.98	49.01	9.56	156
Tarn-et-G.	12.45	38.97	14.05	117
Var	8.61	34.73	4.68	170

Table R (continued)

Department	Yield	% Fallow	% Art. M.	Manure/H
Vaucluse	12.34	53.54	16.37	243
Vendee	11.88	49.37	11.47	160
Vienne	12.47	44.56	22.49	153
Vienne-H.	11.31	57.71	1.07	123
Vosges	18.45	37.97	10.71	183
Yonne	13.46	37.14	28.97	149

[1] 8 crop weighted (by area planted) average

[2] Fallow ÷ 8 crop area + artificial meadows

[3] Artificial meadows ÷ 8 crop area

[4] Average quantity of stable manure used as fertilizer on a hectare of land (in metric quintals)

Sources: Enquête, 1852.

Table S: Specifications of Departmental Variables

Period 1

Variable	Low	High	Mean	Std. Dev.	Variance
BR	20.86	36.84	28.55	3.446	11.875
DR	18.45	29.43	23.96	2.539	6.447
RNI	- 0.75	8.60	4.59	2.040	4.163
RNM	- 4.88	5.44	- 0.09	1.725	2.977
RTI	- 0.10	10.64	4.50	2.216	4.911
RNI_0	1.29	9.11	5.11	1.927	3.715
GRP	- 0.25	28.56	12.72	6.068	36.82
GPR	-12.54	159.84	42.54	33.390	1114.9
GY	- 6.00	87.00	29.47	19.984	399.39
GH	-16.40	126.39	20.32	22.174	491.69
RGH	-14.15	102.99	17.81	20.180	407.24
IY	4.32	24.10	11.44	3.934	15.48
LP	14.05	80.29	51.43	14.737	217.179
RP/U	43.11	167.00	84.19	26.523	703.51
%Ag	23.00	77.00	54.29	12.348	152.49

Period 2

Variable	Low	High	Mean	Std. Dev.	Variance
BR	18.79	33.71	25.61	3.529	12.457
DR	19.90	29.51	23.57	2.065	4.266
RNI	- 2.95	7.88	2.43	2.510	6.300
RNM	- 6.38	5.80	- 1.49	2.340	5.476
RTI	- 5.26	9.97	5.93	3.164	10.008
RNI_1	- 0.75	8.60	4.59	2.040	4.163
GRP	-21.71	17.82	- 2.49	7.637	58.32
GPR	-29.92	136.20	28.80	27.80	772.86
GY	-24.00	83.00	13.82	19.006	361.23
GH	-28.16	43.12	4.62	14.531	211.16
IY	5.11	30.48	14.69	4.810	23.132
LP	- 3.19	79.83	44.61	16.061	257.97
RP/U	46.13	204.91	94.78	30.397	924.00
%Ag	23.00	77.00	54.29	12.348	152.49
TMFR	1.06	2.90	1.81	0.422	0.178
%LIT	53.7	98.4	81.13	10.312	106.35

DISSERTATIONS IN EUROPEAN ECONOMIC HISTORY

An Arno Press Collection

Atkin, John Michael. **British Overseas Investment, 1918-1931** (Doctoral Dissertation, University of London, 1968). 1977

Brosselin, Arlette. **Les Forêts De La Côte D'Or Au XIXème Siècle, et L'Utilisation De Leurs Produits** (Doctoral Thesis, Université de Dijon, 1973). 1977

Brumont, Francis. **La Bureba A L'Époque De Philippe II** (Doctoral Dissertation, Université de Toulouse, 1974). 1977

Cohen, Jon S. **Finance and Industrialization in Italy, 1894-1914** (Doctoral Dissertation, University of California, Berkeley, 1966). 1977

Dagneau, Jacques. **Les Agences Régionales Du Crédit Lyonnais, Années 1870-1914** (Doctoral Thesis, Université de Paris-VIII, 1975). 1977

Dennis, Kenneth G. **'Competition' in the History of Economic Thought** (Doctoral Dissertation, Oxford University, 1975). 1977

Desert, Gabriel. **Une Société Rurale Au XIXe Siècle:** Les Paysans Du Calvados, 1815-1895 (Doctoral Dissertation, Université de Paris, Sorbonne, 1971). 1977

Fierain, Jacques. **Les Raffineries De Sucre Des Ports En France:** XIXe -- début du XXe siècles (Doctoral Dissertation, Université de Nantes, 1974). 1977

Goreux, Louis-Marie. **Agricultural Productivity and Economic Development in France, 1852-1950** (Doctoral Dissertation, University of Chicago, 1955). With the Revised French Version. 1977

Guignet, Philippe. **Mines, Manufactures et Ouvriers Du Valenciennois Au XVIIIe Siècle** (Doctoral Dissertation, Université de Lille III, 1976). Two vols. in one. 1977

Haines, Michael R. **Economic-Demographic Interrelations in Developing Agricultural Regions:** A Case Study of Prussian Upper Silesia, 1840-1914 (Doctoral Dissertation, University of Pennsylvania, 1971). 1977

Hohorst, Gerd. **Wirtschaftswachstum Und Bevölkerungsentwicklung In Preussen 1816 Bis 1914** (Doctoral Dissertation, University of Münster, 1977). 1977

Huertas, Thomas Francis. **Economic Growth and Economic Policy in a Multinational Setting:** The Habsburg Monarchy, 1841-1865 (Doctoral Dissertation, University of Chicago, 1977). 1977

Jankowski, Manfred. **Public Policy in Industrial Growth:** The Case of the Early Ruhr Mining Region, 1766-1865 (Doctoral Dissertation, University of Wisconsin, 1969). 1977

Jefferys, James B. **Business Organisation in Great Britain, 1856-1914** (Doctoral Dissertation, University of London, 1938). 1977

Kirchhain, Günter. **Das Wachstum Der Deutschen Baumwollindustrie Im 19. Jahrhundert** (Doctoral Dissertation, University of Münster, 1973). 1977

Von Laer, Hermann. **Industrialisierung Und Qualität Der Arbeit Eine Bildungsökonomische Untersuchung Für Das 19. Jahrhundert** (Doctoral Dissertation, University of Münster, 1975). 1977

Lee, W. R. **Population Growth, Economic Development and Social Change in Bavaria, 1750-1850** (Revised Doctoral Dissertation, University of Oxford, 1972). 1977

LeVeen, E. Phillip. **British Slave Trade Suppression Policies, 1821-1865** (Doctoral Dissertation, University of Chicago, 1972). 1977

Metzer, Jacob. **Some Economic Aspects of Railroad Development in Tsarist Russia** (Doctoral Dissertation, University of Chicago, 1972). 1977

Moe, Thorvald. **Demographic Developments and Economic Growth in Norway, 1740-1940** (Doctoral Dissertation, Stanford University, 1970). 1977

Mueller, Reinhold C. **The Procuratori di San Marco and the Venetian Credit Market:** A Study of the Development of Credit and Banking in the Trecento (Doctoral Dissertation, Johns Hopkins University, 1969). 1977

Neuburger, Hugh. **German Banks and German Economic Growth from Unification to World War I** (Doctoral Dissertation, University of Chicago, 1974). 1977

Newell, William Henry. **Population Change and Agricultural Developments in Nineteenth Century France** (Doctoral Dissertation, University of Pennsylvania, 1971). 1977

Saly, Pierre. **La Politique Des Grands Travaux En France, 1929-1939** (Doctoral Dissertation, Université de Paris VIII, Vincennes, 1975). 1977

Shrimpton, Colin. **The Landed Society and the Farming Community of Essex in the Late Eighteenth and Early Nineteenth Centuries** (Doctoral Dissertation, Cambridge University, 1965). 1977

Tortella[-Casares], Gabriel. **Banking, Railroads, and Industry in Spain, 1829-1874** (Doctoral Dissertation, University of Wisconsin, 1972). 1977

Viallon, Jean-Baptiste. **La Croissance Agricole En France Et En Bourgogne De 1850 A Nos Jours** (Doctoral Dissertation, Université de Dijon, 1976). 1977

Villiers, Patrick. **Le Commerce Colonial Atlantique Et La Guerre D'Indépendance Des États Unis D'Amérique, 1778-1783** (Doctoral Dissertation, Université de Paris I, Pantheon-Sorbonne, 1975). 1977

Walters, R. H. **The Economic and Business History of the South Wales Steam Coal Industry, 1840-1914** (Doctoral Dissertation, Oxford University, 1975). 1977